LEADERS AN

Leaders and Workers

EDITED BY

J. W. BOYLE

The Thomas Davis Lecture Series

Published in collaboration with
Radio Telefís Éireann
by
THE MERCIER PRESS
Dublin and Cork

The Mercier Press Limited
4 Bridge Street, Cork
25 Lower Abbey Street, Dublin 1

Leaders and Workers
First published 1966
ISBN 0 85342 334 2
© The Mercier Press Limited 1966
This Edition, 1978

The Thomas Davis Lectures
General Editor: Michael Littleton
Every autumn, winter and spring since September 1953, Radio Telefis Eireann has been broadcasting half-hour lectures, named in honour of Thomas Davis. Inspired by one of his famous sayings, 'Educate that you may be free', the aim of these lectures has been to provide in popular form what is best in Irish scholarship and the sciences.

Most of the lectures have been in series; many have been single broadcasts; some have been in English, some in Irish. In the time that has passed since they were initiated, the lectures have dealt with many aspects and with many centuries of Irish social life, history, science and literature. The lectures, distinguished for their special learning at home and abroad, have been drawn from many nations but mainly from Ireland.

A list of the collections of Thomas Davis Lectures available from The Mercier Press is printed in the back of this book.

Printed in Ireland by the Leinster Leader, Naas.

CONTENTS

INTRODUCTION

EVERY autumn, winter, and spring since September 1953, Radio Éireann has been broadcasting half-hour lectures, named in honour of Thomas Davis. Inspired by one of his famous sayings, 'Educate that you may be free,' the aim of these lectures has been to provide in popular form what is best in Irish scholarship and the sciences.

Most of the lectures have been in series; many have been single broadcasts; some have been in English, some in Irish. In the comparatively short time that has passed since they were initiated, the lectures have dealt with many aspects and with many centuries of Irish social life, history, science and literature. The lecturers, distinguished for their special learning at home and abroad, have been drawn from many nations but mainly from Ireland.

The general titles of some of the series provide an idea of the variety and scope of the lectures: Early Irish Society; Saint Patrick; Ireland and Renaissance Europe; Irish Battles; Science and the Nation's Resources; Irish Folklore; The Land and the People; The Shaping of Modern Ireland; The Celts; and The Integrity of Yeats.

FOREWORD

It would require a shelf of no great length to accommodate the volumes that have been published on Irish social and economic history, and a more modest one to take those written on the Irish labour and socialist movement. For America and for most European countries the reader interested in the history of trade unionism, or of radical and socialist thought in his own country, has at his disposal a substantial number of general surveys and specialist studies, a number that is steadily increasing as the growing importance of working-class organisations is acknowledged. The Irish student is less fortunate; a mere handful of books, now out of print or obtainable with difficulty outside libraries, is all that has been added to Connolly's pioneering *Labour in Irish history* in the half-century that has elapsed since its appearance.

It occurred to Mr. Francis MacManus of Radio Éireann that there was room for a series of Thomas Davis lectures on Irish leaders and thinkers of the labour movement, and in consequence he asked me to act as consulting editor. Nine lectures were broadcast during the winter of 1961; they are now printed in this volume, slightly revised in some cases or, where lack of time had required the originals to be shortened, with omitted passages restored.

No finality is claimed either in the canon of subjects or in their treatment; it is proper to add, however, that much of the work is of a pioneer character, based on sources hitherto unutilised.

J. W. BOYLE,
Holywood,
Co. Down

WILLIAM THOMPSON
AND THE SOCIALIST TRADITION

AT FIRST sight, William Thompson, the son of a landlord who had been mayor of Cork, might seem an incongruous figure in any survey of Irish leaders and workers. Yet this man, perhaps unknown to himself, was directly in the social revolutionary tradition of the United Irishmen; he was, certainly, the first Irish socialist and the formulator of economic theories usually associated with Karl Marx. In fact, twenty-three years before the *Communist manifesto* and forty-three years before *Das Kapital*, this un-typical Cork landlord laid the theoretical foundations of modern socialism.

Theobald Wolfe Tone, in his second best-known quotation, wrote: 'Our freedom must be had at all hazards. If the men of property will not help us they must fall; we will free ourselves by the aid of that large and respectable class of the community— the men of no property.' These were Irishmen alive to the plight of men—and women—of no property:—William Thompson, John Doherty, Fergus O'Connor, James Bronterre O'Brien, James Fintan Lalor, Michael Davitt, William Walker, James Connolly and James Larkin. Like Tone before them, they were all concerned with politics, though what chiefly binds them together is their search for a vision into the social and economic relationships of the poor and the dispossessed. All of them were avowed internationalists; with the exception of Walker, they saw, in different ways, the fight of the Irish for freedom as part of the fight of the oppressed everywhere; they identified Ireland's cause with the cause of universal democracy. They had this common bond, but there was no dreary uniformity about them. It is the distinctiveness of their personalities and their humanity that compels our sympathy, together with their common democratic tradition. Not all of them were, themselves, aware that they belonged to the same tradition; indeed, even today, many of us do not see the bond between them, partly because they have had far less than their due from historians. One of them a historian himself, did, with remarkable insight, see that common tradition—James Connolly. After he had written *Labour in Irish history*, nothing before or since in the romantic version of Irish history has had the same significance. He had serious defects as a historian, but the defects were remarkably few: he was sometimes inclined to read too much into general

9

statements, especially if these suggested his own conception of socialism; his greatness rests in his superb intelligence, and in his ability to select the essentials that give historical facts a new and, often, luminous meaning. From the United Irishmen to his own day, he traced the trend of democratic thought and showed how some Irishmen had inspired and nourished it.

The French revolution, 'this gigantic event', according to Wolfe Tone, 'changed in an instant the politics of Ireland.' It became, he adds, 'the test of every man's political creed and the nation was fairly divided into two great parties, the aristocrats and the democrats . . .' The French revolution was, indeed, the inspiration of Wolfe Tone and his fellow members of the United Irishmen; their bible was Tom Paine's *The rights of man*, published in February, 1791 as a reply to Edmund Burke's *Reflections on the French revolution*. It had an immediate and very wide circulation in Ireland as well as in England. Tone could not have foreseen how the seeds sown by the United Irishmen of the social doctrines of the French revolution were soon to produce among Irish emigrants to Lancashire and Yorkshire, a dramatic harvest in the unlikely setting of the English industrial revolution.

Like many other men of humanity and idealism, Wolfe Tone was inspired by the French revolution. Its ideas of liberty aroused him as it did the other United Irishmen. He regarded Tom Paine's *Age of reason* as 'Damned trash!' He was critical of Paine's vanity, not to speak of his absurd theology, when eventually the two men met in Paris in the spring of 1798. Yet he liked Tom Paine, his drinking habits and all, and admitted that Paine had 'done wonders for the cause of liberty both in America and Europe. . . .' Tone had neither the training nor the opportunity to be a consistent social or economic analyst; nevertheless, his political principles were abundantly clear and clearly defined. He himself answered the critics of his apparent inconsistencies in a famous passage, which was probably written in collaboration with, among others, Samuel Neilson on behalf of the Society of United Irishmen:

> It is by wandering from the few plain and simple principles of political faith that our politics, like our religion, has become preaching, not practice; words not works . . . The greatest happiness of the greatest number —on the rock of this principle let this society rest.

After the rising of 1798 the British authorities tried to break the power of the United Irishmen. Great numbers of Ulster men and women emigrated to the north of England and Scotland. At first, they were mainly artisans, whose skill as weavers helped them to find work in the inhospitable cotton mills of Manchester and Glasgow. With the decay of the Irish textile industry after the Union, further waves of emigrants from all parts of Ireland went to Lancashire, Yorkshire and Lanarkshire. In self-defence against the conditions of their work they were quick to organize in trades unions even before the repeal of the Combination Acts in 1824. An Ulsterman, John Doherty, the secretary of the Lancaster cotton spinners' union—the first skilled trade created by the industrial revolution—has a unique place in the history of English trades unionism. The structure of his union is said to have closely resembled the military organization of the United Irishmen. The new Irish industrial workers in England, particularly the handloom weavers, later formed the extreme left wing of the Chartist movement in the eighteen-thirties. One of its middle-class leaders was Fergus O'Connor. He was, perhaps, too much a demagogue, but he converted Chartism in the north of England into a mass movement of working-class democracy. He advocated physical force to the dismay of the moderate and middle-class radicals who also supported Chartism. With another Irishman, Bronterre O'Brien, O'Connor drew up the social content of the Charter, even though the two men differed profoundly on certain issues. O'Connor's utopian solution for the social and human problems of the industrial revolution was a return to the land—under co-operative ownership. It was, however, an intelligible solution, especially to the uprooted Irish peasants who had emigrated to Britain in the later eighteen-thirties. The Chartist movement failed to achieve immediately any one of its aims. Yet, the vision of its leaders, many of them Irish, and the massive fervour of its members shaped in due course the pattern of English politics. It implanted a common political consciousness among the poor and created a working-class solidarity that became part of the socialist tradition in England. In the 1848 rising in Ireland, the social democratic tradition of the United Irishmen was reflected in the attitudes of James Fintan Lalor 'and Thomas Devin Reilly. They had urged that the links between Young Ireland and the Irish landowners could lead only to a futile and mainly middle-class demonstration. With few exceptions, however, the Young Irelanders contemplated a national rising rather than a social democratic revolution.

William Thompson of Cork never met Wolfe Tone, and he would probably have described as irrelevant some of Tone's most cherished political ideals. He would, however, have sympathized with the social and democratic opinions of Tone's closest friends. Thompson was a landowner who championed the cause of the man and woman of no property in Ireland and elsewhere. Though his background had little in common with that of the United Irishmen, he was an exponent, and a most persuasive one, of their economic and social views. He translated their few, simple and often vague, guiding principles into systematically formulated doctrines; and so he became what James Connolly described as the first Irish socialist, and as an economic thinker, the anticipator of some basic theories of Karl Marx.

Thompson was born in Cork in 1775; his family belonged to the protestant ascendancy, the absentee landlord class that then held a monopoly of all state positions, all power and patronage and most of the wealth and education of the country. His father, Alderman John Thompson, a very prosperous Cork merchant, had been mayor of Cork as well as high sheriff of the county. John Thompson died in affluence, and in 1814 his son inherited the lucrative family business which included a fleet of trading vessels as well as the estate of about 1,500 acres at Clonkeen, Roscarbery, some forty miles away, overlooking the beautiful harbour of Glandore.

The son had no interest in adding to the wealth of the family business. His concern was public welfare, not private fortune-making. He lived in a fine house in Patrick Street which had an extensive library. He was a prominent member of the Cork Institution and of the Philosophical, Scientific and Literary Society. Like many other educated and intelligent Irishmen, his thinking had been excited by the French revolution and disturbed by the industrial revolution that was then taking place in England. He had travelled in France and Holland and had been associated with leading French political and economic writers. On public affairs his views were radical and challenging, and he made no effort to conceal them. His catholic tenants may have tolerated his atheism, but his democratic convictions outraged his own class. There is a tradition that, when visiting his estate in poverty-stricken Glandore, he walked about with a French tricolour 'at the end of his walking-stick'. His revolutionary beliefs and his feeling for the poor brought him into conflict with the protestant ascendancy. He particularly affronted them at elections in 1812 and 1826 by supporting Christopher Hely-Hutchinson and catholic emancipation. Soon after becoming proprietor at Glandore he decided to end his career as an absentee landlord. He gave leases on generous terms and introduced improved methods of cultivation. He was widely read in agricultural science and made practical plans for scientific farming and the growing of new root crops by his tenants. His human qualities, his eccentricities and the impact of his personality must have been very considerable. The people of Roscarbery may have been shocked by some of his views; but they judged him by his actions; they remembered him for his humanity and kindness, and admired him for his personal austerity, which for a man of his class caused general astonishment. He was a vegetarian in the latter part of his life and neither smoked nor drank. He used to say that living in this way enabled him to read and write better.

His interest in philosophy made him known to the country people as a magician; he was, in fact, a student of chemistry and frequently lectured on it in Cork. His main concern was to increase the prosperity of the people of Roscarbery and his efforts are still talked about. He was obsessed by a sense of guilt in living on rent, 'the produce of the effort of others' as he called it. 'I am not', he said, 'what is usually called a labourer. Under equitable social arrangements, possessed of health and strength, I ought to blush making this declaration.' He tried to make the Cork Institution a means of providing education, especially for the poor. His particular interest was the social sciences, economics and the philosophy of history, but he also wanted the people to read literature so as to cultivate their taste. His test of education was utility, and so he sometimes ridiculed the time spent on the study of dead languages. He was appalled by the neglect in a commercial city, such as Cork, of a systematic study of the social sciences and practical economics. His quest was for a means of combining human happiness with an industrial age. To do this, he sought a better understanding of economic forces and of their impact on political and social relationships.

Thompson was a close friend and became a life-long disciple of Jeremy Bentham, the English philosopher and founder of the philosophy of utilitarianism. Bentham's social teaching, like that of the United Irishmen was summarized in the slogan— 'the greatest happiness of the greatest number.' His economics came from the classical English economics of David Ricardo. Thompson had been greatly impressed by Jeremy Bentham, especially by his efforts to study human behaviour scientifically. He even declared, somewhat generously, that Bentham 'had done more for moral science than Bacon did for physical science.' The friendship between the two men endured, even though Thompson eventually rejected Bentham's economic doctrines. Thompson was more concerned with the just distribution of wealth than with its accumulation.

He followed Ricardo in arguing that the value of a commodity was equal to the value of the labour that produced it. From this proposition, however, he drew the un-Ricardian conclusion that, in social justice, the labourer was entitled to the full value of his labour. Under capitalism the labourer was paid the lowest wage that the market competition for labour determined. The rest of the produce went to the capitalist in profit and interest. Few explained this 'discovery' so clearly as Thompson, and no one elucidated its economic significance so carefully. It is this exposition of the social right of the worker to the full product of his labour that makes Thompson the founder of 'scientific' socialism and a most important forerunner of Karl Marx.

The concept of surplus value is the fundamental principle of Marxist socialism. There are no grounds, however, for believing that Marx plagiarized Thompson, even though I once thought so myself. Marx was, perhaps, less than generous in his acknowledgements to Thompson in *Das Kapital*—there is only a single, meagre footnote—but Marx's survey of early capitalism was, of course, more comprehensive and penetrating than that of any of his predecessors.

When Thompson rejected Bentham's economics he applied his great friend's utilitarianism to arguments for replacing the capitalist system of the industrial revolution by a commonwealth in which co-operative communities would eliminate surplus value, and with it, capitalism and the profit motive: much later Marx was to reject this voluntary solution. Earlier, however, a society founded on those voluntary lines had been advocated by Robert Owen, a Scottish philanthropist, paternalist factory owner and an enthusiastic exponent of, usually, unrealistic experiments in co-operation.

In 1824 Thompson published a book that he had written while staying with Jeremy Bentham. It had the alarming title of *An inquiry into the principles of distribution of wealth most conducive to human happiness: applied to the newly-proposed system of voluntary equality of wealth*. This remarkable work showed that the co-operative movement had found a leader who far surpassed Robert Owen in his capacity for analysing the structure of society. Thompson's approach was directed towards the masses, not to the few. It was his conviction that the masses could improve themselves only through their own exertions, whereas Owen relied, largely, on appeals to the goodwill of the rich and on aristocratic patronage. Thompson was, I think, the first writer to explain that in the evolution towards socialism the rich as a class would oppose the advance of the majority towards an equalitarian society. 'A few individuals', he said, 'may rise above the impulses of their class . . .' but these would be exceptions, of which, of course, he himself was one. In his assessment of the influence of economic environment on the shaping of political attitudes he was, certainly, a most important forerunner of Karl Marx.

Unlike Marx, Thompson was little attracted by state intervention as a remedy for social and economic injustice. He had seen some state activity in Ireland, and much of it was corrupt. Insofar as he was a communist, his concept of the ideal society was one in which the tyrannical state had withered away. Though a supporter of co-operation, he was, nevertheless, opposed to Robert Owen's belief that appeals to the powerful and wealthy could speed the realization of the co-operative commonwealth. For Thompson, co-operation was a faith for the poor, not a fad for the rich. One can imagine his amused cynicism when the English apostle of co-operation, Robert Owen, came to Dublin in 1822 to canvass the merits of his own socialist and co-operative system, by which Ireland could support a population of fifty millions. Owen addressed his Dublin audience from an improbable platform in the Rotunda that included the archbishop of Dublin, Dr. Troy, the Duke of Leinster, the lord mayor and two peers of the realm. As a result of Owen's persuasiveness, and notwithstanding what some of his audience would regard as his disedifying ideas, there was formed in Dublin the 'Hibernian Philanthropic Society'. The society was not destined to survive; but one of its members, Arthur Vandaleur, a Clare landlord, was so impressed by what he had heard that he immediately converted his estate at Ralahine into a co-operative colony. The colony prospered until 1833 when the bankruptcy of Vandaleur, unable to pay his gambling debts, enabled his creditors to disband the socialist experiment of Ralahine.

In 1830 Thompson published his most important work on co-operation. Its ample title described its aim and scope— *Practical directions for the speedy and economic establishment of communities, on the principle of mutual co-operation, united possessions, equality of exertions and of the means of enjoyment:* This was an amazing publication, intensely practical and covering the subject in minute detail. It was intended as a gospel of co-operative political economy, and unlike other socialist works of the period, it recognised the possibilities for human happiness of the industrial revolution, if society could be properly organized and directed. It insisted that, even in agriculture, there could be no return to the pre-industrial way of life.

Towards the end of his days Thompson began the formation of a co-operative community under his own management on his estate near Roscarbery. He drafted a constitution for the community; it provided for complete freedom of thought and expression 'on all subjects guided by regard for the feelings of others.' Religion was to be a private concern. Women were to be eligible for 'advancement' to all offices, to which their talents and inclinations might lead them. Idlers and 'persons with vicious tendencies would, if deemed irreclaimable by mild treatment', be discharged promptly from the community. He died, however, before his ambitious plans could be completed; only the stone foundations of the experiment survive in Roscarbery. But Thompson was more than a great socialist theoretician, and a leading figure in the co-operative movement; he was also an early and most vigorous advocate of the emancipation of women. In this campaign he had a remarkable ally and engaging collaborator in Anna Wheeler, the daughter of an Irish protestant archbishop and a godchild of Henry Grattan. Between them they produced an attack on the political, social and economic disabilities of women and what they described as 'the rightlessness' of wives against their husbands. Indeed, it was so challenging that it startled even their own radical supporters. The title of this most influential work on feminism— a reply to a famous essay of James Mill—leaves the prospective reader in no doubt as to its contents: *An appeal of one-half of the human race, women, against the pretentions of the other half, men, to retain them in political and thence in civil and domestic slavery.*

Thompson died in 1833 at the age of 58 and was buried in Drumbeg near Glandore. Despite the atheist convictions of the deceased, a nephew, who expected to be his heir, insisted on a religious funeral. When Thompson's will was read, however, there was consternation; the heir apparent was left nothing, as most of the estate was bequeathed to the co-operative movement. Thompson's relatives, faced with a philanthropic scattering of what they regarded as their money, naturally contested the will on various grounds at various stages. They sought to have it set aside on the plea that the testator had been insane, or, alternatively, that the aims of the will 'distinctly showed an intention to abolish marriage', and, consequently, should not be recognised by the courts. The case dragged on for more than twenty-five years and the lawyers became the chief beneficiaries. Even the whereabouts of all Thompson's mortal remains are uncertain. As a gesture against the public prejudice that then existed towards dissection he had requested in his will that his body 'be publicly examined by a lecturer on anatomy' and that the skeleton be preserved in the museum of the first co-operative community established in Great Britain or Ireland. A local doctor named Donovan did exhume the body, and a French phrenologist is believed to have got the cranium. Dr. Donovan later asserted that the body had been bequeathed to him on condition that the bones should be sent to Thompson's friend, Anna Wheeler, 'as a memento of love.'

William Thompson is largely and undeservedly forgotten, though he has found an admirable biographer in Richard Pankhurst, himself a product of crusading stock. Yet, Thompson's place in international socialist thought and in the social democratic tradition in Ireland deserves to be put in its proper setting and perspective. Irishmen and women, at least, should recall the Cork landlord, who, like the United Irishmen, supported the people of no property; and who, in addition, furnished an important footnote, at least, to the history of economic thought wherever and by whom it is written.

PATRICK LYNCH.

JOHN DOHERTY

JOHN DOHERTY is not one of the best-known of the early nineteenth century trade union leaders. Very little has been written about him, yet he is undoubtedly one of the most important, his name appearing again and again in many of the accounts of early trade unionism. Furthermore, he is the first of a long line of Irish emigrants who, as leaders, took a major part in the building of the British labour movement. Doherty's aim, in the words of James Connolly, was 'to organise the working class and to teach them to act on their own initiative'.

Trade unionism was only in its infancy when John Doherty became one of its leaders; indeed, when he joined the Manchester cotton spinners' union in 1817 trade unionism was illegal. Members could be, and were, sent to jail under the combination laws, passed in 1800, forbidding workmen to organise, but prison sentences were not sufficient to deter the pioneers.

Doherty arrived in Manchester in 1817. We know that he came from Ireland because in his evidence years later to a select committee on combinations he stated that he had been born in Buncrana (Donegal) in 1799. In 1814 he was working in a cotton factory near Larne, where he probably learned his trade as a spinner. Though power spinning of cotton was well established in the north of Ireland it was less developed than in Lancashire, where it attracted thousands of Irish workers, including Doherty. Constant work and higher wages were the principal inducements.

When Doherty arrived in Manchester the Lancashire cotton spinners were making their first attempt to set up a united trade union under the title of the Philanthropic Society. Its curious name was probably chosen to make the authorities believe it was a friendly society, since such associations, unlike trade unions, were not illegal. We cannot determine from the scanty records of the short-lived Philanthropic Society whether Doherty was one of its leaders, but it is probable that the society served as a model in his attempt to form trade unions on a national rather than a local basis, though he was also indebted to other organizations. When he appeared in 1838 before the select committee on combinations he told O'Connell that he had taken the pattern for mass trade unionism from the Liberator's own catholic emancipation movement.

By 1819, little more than a year after the Philanthropic Society

had been formed and had faded away, John Doherty had
become the recognised leader of the Manchester cotton spinners.
In January of that year James Norris, one of the magistrates of
Manchester, wrote to inform Lord Sidmouth, who was the
British home secretary, that 'John Doherty was also indicted
for conspiring with others', as Norris put it, 'to intimidate
persons from working at Messrs. Ewart and Co.'s cotton
factory.' Doherty was found guilty and sentenced to two years'
imprisonment in Lancaster Castle.

At that time Doherty was still a very young man, not much
more than twenty when he was sentenced. How the authorities
treated prisoners they were afraid of can be learned from the
case of Henry Hunt, who was given two-and-a-half years for
his part in the Peterloo demonstration in Manchester in 1820.
'Hunt's treatment', wrote the author of the life of Sir Francis
Burdett, 'was barbarous. He was confined to a solitary cell,
dank, dark, and unventilated. The water was contaminated with
the sewage. He was not allowed to see his relations, his solicitor,
or his doctor'. Doherty's treatment in jail can hardly have been
better than that of 'Orator' Hunt.

In the early eighteen-twenties the movement for the repeal of
the combination laws was starting. Trade unionists, quite
naturally, had always regarded these laws as unjust; but the
long war with Napoleon and the fear of plebian movements
that the war put into the hearts of the English ruling classes only
strengthened parliament's belief that trade unionism should not
be allowed. Francis Place, known in trade union history as 'the
radical tailor of Charing Cross' was the organising genius behind
the movement for repeal.

Although Place himself was not a member of parliament he
was able to win the support of such influential people as Joseph
Hume, the radical M.P., and J. R. McCulloch (then editor of
the *Scotsman*), later to make a name for himself as an economist.

But Place also had the support of the trade union leaders in
the industrial towns—men like John Gast, the leader of the
London shipyard workers, and John Doherty, who by this time
(about 1823) was well known as the leader of the Lancashire
cotton workers.

Francis Place directed the campaign so skilfully that parliament repealed the combination laws in 1824, though some of the
employers believed that parliament had been hoodwinked by
Place's manoeuvring. They said, for example, that he packed
the committee the house of commons set up to examine the
combinations, loaded the questions to suit his case, and made
sure that only witnesses favourable to repeal appeared before
the committee.

In 1825 the employers were clamouring for the combination

laws to be re-enacted. Doherty wrote to warn Place that any attempt to re-enact the combination laws would create a widespread revolutionary movement in the industrial districts. In the eighteen-thirties Doherty somewhat modified his idea of trade unionism's aims; but this letter to Place shows that at least in the eighteen-twenties he was a most determined and militant man. The radical tailor himself believed that with the repeal of the combination laws the trade unions would fade away. 'Combinations,' he wrote to Sir Francis Burdett in 1825, 'will soon cease to exist. Men have been kept together for long periods only by the oppression of the laws.'

But John Doherty had other ideas about the future of trade unionism, he saw, not the withering away of the trade union movement, but its growth into a great national body. Trade unions in their early days were local and scattered societies, and organising skill, communications and transport were all insufficiently developed to sustain national organisations. There was as yet no penny post, and the cumbersome and expensive stage coach had not been displaced by the railway.

Despite these handicaps John Doherty started to organise bigger trade unions soon after parliament had repealed the combination laws. In 1828 he appealed for unity to an organization of spinners he called The Imperial Union, though nothing more than the name is known about this body. In the same year, 1828, he started a publication called the *Conciliator;* it was to be the first of many working-class newspapers he was associated with. Doherty was also a pioneer of labour journalism.

The following year (1829) the Manchester cotton spinners started what turned out to be a long and bitter strike over wages. The employers tried to cut the rates and the workers withdrew their labour. John Doherty saw his opportunity to start building in earnest the national union of all spinners that was his aim; in September, 1829 he started the Grand General Union of Spinners. The setting up of this new union was, however, only the prelude to the conference that he called two months later in the Isle of Man. He chose the Isle of Man, he later explained, because it was the geographical centre of these islands. He wanted to bring the Irish and the Scottish cotton workers into one union with the Lancashire cotton workers.

From this conference there emerged the Grand General Union of Operative Spinners of Great Britain and Ireland with its controlling committee in Manchester. This was the first union to which textile workers in the three countries all belonged and it was without doubt a most ambitious venture. The cotton spinners of Belfast must have sent someone to this conference because most of the discussion centred round whether or not there should be one executive council or three separate committees, one each for England, Scotland and Ireland. In the end they decided in favour of one council.

The Grand General Union asked its members to pay a penny a week; its main purpose, apart from establishing fair wages, was to agitate for the legal control of hours and working conditions in the factories, workers then being more concerned about factory legislation than about trade unionism as such. In 1819, for example, when the pressure against the unions was very strong the spinners of Manchester dropped out of the union but kept paying into the funds of the movement for factory reform. The improvement of factory conditions was another of John Doherty's main objects. Meanwhile he became general secretary of the new cotton spinners' union.

The Grand General Union of Cotton Spinners was not, however, the end of the road for John Doherty. He had not given up his dream of a union of all the trades; and in 1830 after long discussions with twenty other trade unions he launched the National Association for the Protection of Labour. He resigned from the secretaryship of the cotton spinners' union to lead the new association.

The National Association for the Protection of Labour was in reality an early form of what is now the Trades Union Congress, though the British T.U.C. was not started until 1868, nearly forty years later. The National Association for the Protection of Labour was not simply a federation of kindred workers engaged in a single industry, it was an association of several different trades combining the workers in many industries. Soon about 150 different unions had joined the National Association, including not only unions in the various textile trades but also unions of engineers, iron moulders and blacksmiths and of numerous other trades—a grand total, it has been estimated, of up to 20,000.

The National Association for the Protection of Labour with John Doherty as its leader also formed unions in places and industries where there had been no unions before. It was Doherty himself, for example, who started a union for the Staffordshire pottery workers. Coal miners also joined the National Association. Early in 1831 9,000 miners from the counties of Staffordshire, Yorkshire and Cheshire, and from parts of North Wales too came into the new organization. Soon after this the trade unions in Belfast applied for affiliation—and were no doubt admitted. So it would probably be no exaggeration to say that less than a year after it started the National Association for the Protection of Labour had an affiliated membership of about 100,000.

At the beginning of 1831 John Doherty started his most famous newspaper, the *Voice of the People*, published weekly in

Manchester and edited by himself. The *Voice of the People* was in effect the newspaper of the National Association for the Protection of Labour; it was by no means an insignificant working-class journal, on the contrary it was a full-sized newspaper, as big as the *Manchester Guardian* and just as well laid out. The *Manchester Guardian* was itself a good newspaper because it was the organ of the industrialists and middle-class radicals who were demanding the reform of parliament.

Despite its obvious working-class bias Doherty's paper was patronised by such advertisers as book-publishers and coaching companies. Employers invited its readers to apply for important jobs, one firm, for instance, advertised for a manager 'capable of running an entire fustian factory'. In 1831 the Bank of Manchester published a full report of its annual meeting in its columns. Among its correspondents and contributors were O'Connell and the well-known radical, William Cobbett, who wrote an article in which he denounced a plan to encourage mass emigration. It carried foreign as well as home news.

Not unexpectedly, every issue of the paper contained reports from Ireland, protests about the revival of the Orange movement in the north, or rack-renting and distress in Mayo, or the story of some sad disaster like that in which two poor Irish weavers were refused permission to land in Bristol and died of starvation aboard the ship where the parish settlement officers put them.

The *Voice of the People* denounced the pernicious truck system which allowed some employers to rob the factory hands of their hard-earned wages; it supported the movement for the reform of parliament; called consistently for factory legislation; and even organised public meetings. At one of these William Thompson of Cork, economist, co-operator and precursor of Marx, gave a lecture on co-operation.

By the autumn of 1831 the National Association for the Protection of Labour was firmly established in the northern counties of England. Doherty advised the Manchester committee controlling the association that they should get in touch with London so that a completely national movement of all trades could be started and proposed that the offices of the *Voice of the People* be transferred to London. His plan was to advance step by step towards national trade union unity. Firstly he united the cotton spinners, when he called the Isle of Man conference; then he united the various trades in the northern industrial counties by setting up the National Association; now he wished to bring in the London trade unions. Had he succeeded the trade union movement in Britain would have been firmly established as a national movement, with its own newspaper and perhaps its own political party in the eighteen-thirties because Doherty, like his friend Robert Owen, was a socialist. But the mission to London failed. Doherty was unable to enlist the support of Cobbett and Place or to persuade a printer to publish the *Voice of the People;* even his attempt to form a London committee of the National Association for the Protection of Labour was unsuccessful. In the autumn of 1831 the radicals of London were more interested in the reform bill then before both houses of parliament than in Doherty's plans for national trade union unity.

So Doherty returned to Manchester a disappointed man, to find that his comrades in the National Association had prepared a list of accusations against him. The gist of these charges was that Doherty had failed to do what he set out to do in London and that his expenses for the journey were too high. In view of these accusations and because of the bad feeling there must have been in the Manchester committee Doherty withdrew from the National Association for the Protection of Labour—and soon afterwards that organization faded out of history.

Doherty himself may not have been an easy man to work with. Francis Place once called him 'a hot-headed Roman Catholic', though that was because Place disliked him. Place was a political manoeuvrer, Doherty was an impatient reformer who wanted swift and sweeping changes in the conditions of life of the industrial workers. The Webbs in their *History of trade unionism* say that he 'was one of the acutest thinkers and stoutest leaders . . . of his time'. Yet it is probably true that Doherty was hot-headed. His letter to Place in 1825 predicting industrial revolution if the combination laws were re-enacted reveals, in a way, what kind of a man he was. And in January, 1831 when he went to a dinner in honour of Henry Hunt, who had been elected radical M.P. for Preston, he apologised for having offended somebody at an earlier meeting. It seems as if he did lose his temper at times.

When he left the National Association for the Protection of Labour, John Doherty turned to the newly formed Society for Promoting National Regeneration. This curiously-named body was really a movement to establish a shorter working day in the factories. Doherty and other working-class leaders, and even some of the more humane and enlightened employers, were exasperated because the government and parliament were doing little to improve factory conditions. The first factory act had been passed in 1801 but it applied only to pauper boys in cotton mills. Another act was passed in 1819 but it too fell far short of what the workers were asking for; many of the employers ignored this law because there were no factory inspectors to enforce it. Doherty, who had always been interested in factory reform, wanted to stop the employment of little children, then widespread in all the industrial districts, and to have the hours of work restricted by law. At that time the adult factory workers, and in many cases the children too, worked excessively long hours, often twelve or fourteen hours a day for six days a week.

The Society for Promoting National Regeneration aimed to reduce these long hours, not just by asking parliament to pass a law but by the more direct method of advising all factory workers to do no more than an eight-hour day on and from 1st March, 1834. The society was taking the advice of Lord Althorpe who said that the cotton workers should 'make a short-time bill for themselves', they should, in other words, knock off work and go home when they had finished their eight hours.

But this was easier said than done. The society was in touch with only a very small number of workers, and even these would have found it difficult to know when the eight were up. None of the factories in those days had clocks, the employer himself saying when the work should stop. The workers would hardly notice an extra ten or fifteen minutes, especially as many of them were children who could not read the clock even if there had been one. The Society for Promoting National Regeneration, therefore, got little support. The industrial workers did not understand it, and the more orthodox factory reformers—the people who preferred to work through petitions and parliament—thought that walking out at the end of the eight hours would do more harm than good.

Nevertheless, the idea that the factory workers should take matters into their own hands or—to put it another way—should vote for the eight-hour day with their feet, appealed to John Doherty, just as it appealed to Robert Owen. Owen had by this time a world-wide reputation as a socialist, a co-operator, and a reformer. He had pioneered enlightened factory management in Scotland and had spent a fortune trying to promote voluntary co-operative communities in the United States. After this he came back to England where he threw all his enthusiasm, his great sincerity, and his extraordinary genius for organising into the trade union movement. Owen and Doherty, for the brief period they worked together, must have been a remarkable pair of leaders. They formed a partnership that was very like the partnership of Connolly and Larkin in the Irish trade union movement.

The reform act of 1832 removed some of the worst defects of parliament and widened democracy a little, but only a little. The act was a great disappointment to John Doherty and indeed to all the working class leaders of that time; they had fully expected that industrial workers would be included in the new franchise—

one of the reformers Doherty had campaigned for when he was editor of the *Voice of the People*.

The exclusion of the industrial workers from the reform act and the Poor Law Amendment Act of 1834 were two of the events that led to the Chartist agitation in the late eighteen-thirties. But Doherty, strangely enough, took no part in the Chartist movement even though it was led by two other Irishmen, Fergus O'Connor and Bronterre O'Brien.

By 1834 Doherty had started business as a printer and book-seller in Manchester, retaining some connections with the working-class movement. He continued to work for factory reform even though factory reform was for a time overshadowed by the Chartist movement. And he lived to see parliament pass the ten-hour bill in 1847.

In 1838 Doherty appeared before a select committee, which included O'Connell, on combinations of workmen. In his evidence Doherty summed up the aims of the trade unions as resistance to wage cuts, reduction of the working day to ten hours or less, the prevention of the harsh treatment of factory workers. The whole of Doherty's long evidence before this committee is noteworthy for its sincerity, intelligence, and consistency.

One interesting thing about this remarkable Irish emigrant was his attitude to the use of machinery. The Luddites wrecked machines, thereby risking death on the scaffold, because they were afraid their labour would be no longer required; Doherty, industrial worker though he himself was, looked at this problem in a different way. He argued that if men had never invented tools and machines they would never have raised their standards of living. In a remarkably prophetic article in the *Voice of the People* he defended the use of machines because he believed this would eventually free men from physical toil:

> If machines could be so constructed as to convey us to any part of the globe with the utmost dispatch, no one could question their advantage. Most men would agree that if machines could be invented to do all the work that man requires to be done a great benefit would be conferred on the human race.

Doherty himself, if we are to judge from these views, would have been quite happy in this age of automation, nuclear energy, and jet travel. But he lived in an age when even mass production was in a primitive stage. In his day he strove to introduce some humanity into industry, and he did this through the trade unions he pioneered, through the co-operative movement of which he was one of the first members, through factory legislation and through the reform of parliament.

Doherty's work was not in vain. He was perhaps ahead of the times but much of what he aimed for has since been achieved. The trade unions are now not only great national but also great international organisations. Organisations like the British T.U.C. and the Irish Congress of Trade Unions are the realization of John Doherty's dream of a union of all the trades. In all advanced countries a vast number of beneficial laws protect the health and welfare of factory workers. Parliamentary democracy has given the vote to every adult. These were the reforms John Doherty advocated nearly a century-and-a-half ago.

When Doherty died in Manchester in 1854 Lord Shaftesbury said he 'was the most faithful to a cause that ever lived'. And that tribute, coming as it did from the man whose name will always be linked with the emancipation of the factory workers, is a truer description of John Doherty than Francis Place's ill-tempered remark about his being 'a hot-headed Roman Catholic'.

ANDREW BOYD.

FERGUS O'CONNOR AND J. BRONTERRE O'BRIEN

CHARTISM WAS one of the most exciting, interesting and significant social movements of modern times. In the summer and autumn of 1838, a year of economic gloom and general discontent, workingmen in many different parts of England, Scotland and Wales banded themselves together to fight for the People's Charter, a document which would give them a full say in the country's affairs—the right to vote, the right to send their own members to parliament without qualifications of property, and the power to change the economic and social policies of the country. The battle continued with varying degrees of intensity for more than ten years until it finally petered out—with its objects still not accomplished—in the more quiet middle years of the nineteenth century.

At the end of the century the makers of the labour movement saw Chartism as a preliminary initiation into mass organization, a precursor of their own parties and institutions. In the middle of the twentieth century we can see it as a stirring phase in a great social and political awakening, a turbulent struggle to assert basic social rights through the use of political machinery, yet a movement at the same time pulled back and pushed forward, with curious parallels in more recent societies in quite different parts of the world.

Two Irishmen played a key part in the Chartist story, although their roles, like their personalities, were quite different. Fergus O'Connor, born in 1794 (or 1796), the son of the wild Roger O'Connor, who claimed descent from the ancient kings of Ireland, was certainly the king of the Chartists. There was a messianic strain in his appeal. Passionate, generous, sometimes unreliable, ultimately mad, O'Connor reflected almost every facet of Chartism at various stages of his adventurous but committed career. Indeed he was so much the embodiment of Chartism, with all its strengths and weaknesses, that he failed to provide it with the kind of skilled leadership—independent, calculating and, when occasion demanded, detached—that all his many critics, then and since, have argued might have led the movement to success.

In fact it is very difficult to see how, given the nature of English society and government in the Chartist period, the Chartists could have succeeded in the way that O'Connor's critics claim that they might have done. The cards were too

heavily stacked against them. Both Chartism and O'Connor in
my view were doomed to failure, and it may plausibly be
argued that O'Connor gave the movement a greater measure of
success than otherwise it would have had. An independent
leader would never have been able to identify himself with the
working-class crowds of the north of England as successfully
as O'Connor did. A man who had been less of a demagogue
would never have successfully challenged the dominion of
local radical leaders, and converted Chartism from a series of
local disturbances into a concerted national movement of
agitation and protest. And although Chartism did fail in its
immediate objectives, almost all its political objectives (with the
exception of annual parliaments) were ultimately granted, and
its social objectives were to be taken up later on—many of
them quite successfully—after a long period of political ap-
prenticeship. The defeat of Chartism was ultimately to be
followed by what has been called 'the victory of the vanquished.'

O'Connor's weaknesses, confusions, above all his passionate
feelings were the weaknesses, confusions and feelings of
Chartism as a whole. Bronterre O'Brien, the second Irishman in
the story, born eleven years after O'Connor in 1805, was not
prepared to rest content with these weaknesses. He was a good
Chartist in that he believed, as passionately as any of his
comrades, in the objectives for which the movement was
fighting, but he was a critical Chartist, eventually bitterly
critical of O'Connor, because unlike O'Connor, he thought
clearly, looked for theories to support actions, and always
considered tactics as well as principles. O'Connor called him
'the Chartist schoolmaster', and so in a very real sense he was.
For he tried to guide and to mould Chartism rather than to
take it just as it was. He failed in this attempt at least as decisively
as O'Connor failed in his attempt, but again the failure was a
relative one. His thinking led him to original and fascinating
conclusions, so that what he wrote still bears reading nearly a
hundred years after his death. The spell which O'Connor cast
over the Chartist crowds can only be re-captured in the imagination; the arguments which O'Brien advanced can still be
pondered in the mind.

How did these two Irishmen become Chartists at a time when
the great liberator Daniel O'Connell was extremely suspicious
of left-wing elements in English radicalism? In the case of
O'Connor, part, though not all, of the answer lies in a personal
antagonism between O'Connell and the young and ambitious
politician. O'Connor had been returned to parliament by the
electors of County Cork in 1832 after playing virtually no part
in the catholic emancipation battles of the eighteen-twenties.
Within a few weeks of his entering the house of commons there

were noticeable differences of opinion between him and his leader, O'Connell. 'If our great general will not lead the little band to the fight', O'Connor told the men of Cork at a public dinner in 1833, 'I will'. His chances of doing this effectively were greatly reduced after the general election of 1835. He retained his seat but was dispossessed by petition on the grounds that he had lacked the requisite freehold qualifications to sit as a county member.

From this time onwards O'Connor hitched his political career to England, not to Ireland, although he tried to make a special appeal to the large numbers of Irish immigrants in England and was always a passionate supporter of repeal of the Union. Within a few days of losing his Irish seat he announced that he would stand for Oldham, the constituency which William Cobbett had represented from 1832 until his death. This was not a popular or tactful move since Cobbett's son had already been adopted as a radical candidate. But it pushed O'Connor into the turbulent industrial politics of the north of England.

His final break with the Great Liberator came in the summer of 1836. Increasingly O'Connell had been following a line of argument in parliament which brought him into closer relationship with the whigs. The so-called Lichfield House Compact of February 1835 had guaranteed the whigs the support of Irish votes, and O'Connell agreed with official whig policy on three of the most controversial, economic and political issues of the day—their new poor law of 1834, their opposition to trade unions, and their distrust for the Ten Hours agitation. O'Connor detested whiggery in all its manifestations, cared little for elaborate parliamentary tactics, vigorously criticised the new poor law, and supported the case of the trade unions. Quite apart from personal ambition, therefore, he had many reasons for quarrelling with O'Connell. Once they did quarrel, however, every personal factor was brought into their antagonism. Early in 1837 a virulent pamphlet appeared called *A series of letters from Fergus O'Connor . . . to Daniel O'Connell.* O'Connor made a plea in this pamphlet for a united agitation of Irish peasants and English industrial workers to right the wrongs of both. He made this plea all his life. More significant in practice, however, was his slashing attack on O'Connell as a self-interested dictator who used Irish grievances to buttress his own income and reputation. 'You know you hate me,' O'Connor told O'Connell. 'You know I despise you.'

Fergus went on in England to become the leader of Chartism: O'Connell until his death in 1847 urged the Irish in England as well as the Irish in Ireland to have nothing to do with either Chartism or O'Connor. This breach robbed Chartism of one of its strongest possible instruments of action—Irish discontent.

It was not until after O'Connell's death, and then never in a completely enthusiastic alliance, that Irish nationalists joined hands with English agitators.

In the meantime O'Connor became increasingly a leader of the English discontents. He addressed large public meetings in the north of England and in London, attacking the poor law, favouring factory legislation, supporting the trade unionists of Glasgow and London, and in November 1837, launching the *Northern Star*, a newspaper which soon had a circulation of over ten thousand copies a week, more than the circulation of either the *Leeds Mercury* or the *Manchester Guardian*. He could not be ignored as a fiery political force. Even before he turned, with outstanding success, to address the English crowds a political commentator said of him: 'He is a man of more than respectable talents and though at the moment I write he be not a member of the house of commons, from the circumstances under which he was unseated and his popularity among the radicals in England as well as Ireland, there is little chance of his being long excluded.' The commentator went on to give an account of O'Connor's appearance and oratory at this time:

> In person he is moderately tall, and of a firm compact make, without anything approaching to corpulency. He is red-haired and of very fair complexion. There is a slight protusion in his brow, which gives that part of his face about the eyes somewhat of a sunken or retiring appearance. His nose is prominent, not from its size, which is rather small, but from its cocked-up conformation. He is yet but a young man, his age being about forty . . . he is a fluent and graceful speaker: the chief blemish in his speeches is that they are generally too wordy. His voice has something of a bass tone in it; he cannot modulate or alter it. He is a man of sterling integrity in his public character.

This favourable picture, written by a man who had few axes to grind, was misleading, of course, in suggesting that O'Connor would soon be back in parliament. He did not return to parliament again until 1847, and his career there proved short and disastrous. Yet his appearance and even his wordiness, the only quality of his which was unfavourably commented upon, were assets to him when he chose to appeal not to members of parliament but to northern factory operatives. He was already well-known in the north and his paper widely read when the People's Charter was published in London in May 1838.

Equally important, he had already by this stage quarrelled with some of the men who had taken the initiative in drafting and publishing the Charter, notably William Lovett, the quiet and industrious secretary of the London Working Men's

Association, which had been founded in 1836. Lovett and O'Connor, both pledged to radical reform in the name of the working classes, were poles apart. Lovett wanted a small directorate of politically conscious, intelligent and responsible working men, organising a genuinely democratic movement: O'Connor wanted to collect every man and woman who was discontented, whether literate or illiterate, drunk or sober. Lovett hated demagogy and personal ambition; O'Connor regarded both as quite natural mainsprings of effective political mobilization. Their quarrel was as natural and as bitter as the quarrel between O'Connor and O'Connell. It began two years before the publication of the Charter, with O'Connor branding the London Working Men's Association as 'sham radicals' and 'tools of the whigs'. It reached its climax with a scathing attack on O'Connor by Lovett:

> Your own vain self must be supreme—you must be 'the leader of the people'; you have christened public meetings 'great associations' to meet your purposes—you have declared yourself 'the missionary of all the radicals of London', your constituents being your own presumptuous boastings . . . You carry your fame about with you on all occasions to sink all the other topics in the shade. You are the great I AM of politics.

This bitter indictment shows how unpopular O'Connor was with the very man who took the initiative in drafting the Charter. Yet Lovett could no more stop O'Connor from becoming the Chartist leader than O'Connell could stop him from becoming an English politician. Very cleverly O'Connor used Lovett's attacks against him as a means of rallying support outside London. He deliberately appealed not to the politically conscious, intelligent and responsible section of the working men but to those whom he called 'the fustian jackets and the unshorn chins'. He encouraged the crowds to flirt with the ideas not of moral but of physical force. 'Before joining the union', he told the crowds who flocked to meetings of the Great Northern Union in April 1838, 'every member should distinctly understand that in the event of moral force failing to procure privileges . . . it is resolved that physical force shall be resorted to if necessary'. There was a powerful element of bluff in this statement, for he did not like physical force and was very careful to avoid being too committed even to detailed and specific talk of its use, yet the bluff was no handicap to him in establishing his reputation as a militant and aggressive national leader.

Equally cleverly, O'Connor immediately accepted the People's Charter as if it were his own, and known everywhere as the 'Apostle of the North' carried it to the platforms of

Lancashire and the West Riding. He declared that the Great Northern Union was similar in purpose to the famous radical Birmingham Political Union which had been revived in May 1837. He used his commanding position in the north to make converts in other places, appearing on public platforms whenever and wherever he could, either with other prominent figures or with enthusiastic local Chartists. He began more and more to underline his special qualifications for leading the new movement. 'I would never accept place, pension or employment from any government', he exclaimed, 'save that which was elected by universal suffrage. I am the unpaid, undeviating, unpurchasable friend of liberty, and servant of the people'. With talk of this kind and appeals for resolute action O'Connor won support in places where there were already well established local radical or even Chartist rivals. He beat Lovett in London, and even more significantly Attwood in Birmingham. When the famous People's Parliament, 'the General Convention of the Industrious Classes', met in London in February 1839, O'Connor was indubitably the best known Chartist and many of the delegates felt an intense personal loyalty to him.

One of the delegates at the convention was Bronterre O'Brien. How had he become a Chartist? Like O'Connor he had started as a would-be lawyer, spending six years at Trinity College, Dublin, where he won the Science Medal, and entering Gray's Inn in 1829 with a view to practising at the English Bar. Oddly enough O'Connor had registered at Gray's Inn three years before. O'Brien decided to stay in London, however, where he very quickly abandoned interest in the law in the exciting atmosphere of the pre-reform bill capital. 'My friends', he wrote later, 'sent me to London to study law. I took to radical reform on my own account . . . I soon got sick of law, and gave all my soul to radical reform'. He met Cobbett and Hunt in London, began writing articles for radical papers, read widely in radical literature, including the works of the utopian socialist, Robert Owen. After a spell as a radical newspaper editor in the most radical of English cities, Birmingham, he became editor of the *Poor Man's Guardian* in November 1832. This paper, the leading unstamped paper of the day, issued in defiance of the law, remains a fascinating social and political document. It urged the case for both political and social reform, relying on searching social analysis for its conclusions about current action. A transformation of society, which both he and the Owenites believed to be necessary depended, he argued, on the conquest of political power. Power problems could not be evaded by socialists; they had to be thought about at least as carefully as the social objectives of politics which provided a spur and an inspiration. O'Brien widened his knowledge and deepened his arguments by looking at historical power struggles in other places, particularly in revolutionary France.

He was elected as honorary member of the London Working Men's Association in 1836, and published the manifestoes of the Association and the first draft of the People's Charter in his paper. Like O'Connor, however, he quarrelled with Lovett and his group and was drawn increasingly into the left-wing of London radical politics. His quarrel was concerned also with O'Connell, for he regarded O'Connell's views on trade unionism as being the chief course of confusion in current radicalism. This quarrel, a bitter one, led him naturally into close association with O'Connor, and it was not surprising that O'Connor asked him to write regularly for the *Northern Star*. He established a far greater national reputation through the *Northern Star* than he had ever been able to do before, not least because he provided a vigorous intellectual underpinning for the more emotional declarations of O'Connor. He criticised, for example, Lovett's preoccupation with moral force as the sole method of working for the Charter, and wrote with what even his opponents called 'great dexterity' on the relationship between political reform and social justice. When the People's Convention met, O'Brien was a delegate not only of London, where he had first made his mark as a radical, but of several provincial districts. He made his first speech at the convention, opposing the election of Lovett as secretary, and he was quick to urge the delegates to work out a plan of 'ulterior measures' which would be put into effect if parliament did not accede to the Chartists' demands.

This was the high water-mark of O'Brien's relationship with O'Connor. They had both become Chartists because they sympathised with the discontents of the working classes of industrial England and perhaps even more basically because they both refused to follow political tactics laid down by O'Connell. They had taken up 'extreme positions' which they knew would alienate not only conservatives but a substantial number of moderate radicals. This did not worry them, however, because they believed that only militant action could accomplish great objectives. In O'Brien's case the great objective was a basic social transformation; in the case of O'Connor it was something more vague; the restoration of social justice, perhaps through a return to relationships associated not with factory industry but with peasant agriculture.

These differences of ultimate objective were to become much clearer in the eighteen-forties. Before they became clear, however, the careers and aspirations of the two men had diverged. Yet another Chartist quarrel broke the harmony of a movement pledged to union and solidarity. The quarrel was not about ultimate objectives, but about tactics and the right way to deciding them. Like all quarrels, it became mixed up with personal differences.

There had been signs of a different approach to tactics while the Convention was sitting, although O'Connor and O'Brien succeeded in working in apparent harmony at crucial times. The difference became marked in 1841, when O'Brien was in prison for seditious speeches delivered during the aftermath of the convention, which had broken up in disunity and failure in September 1839. O'Connor, who was also in prison from March 1840 to September 1841 urged Chartists to support tory candidates at the 1841 election, in order to take their revenge on the whigs, whom he had always detested. O'Brien claimed that it was the business of Chartists to 'disavow both factions alike'. If this seemed an extreme point of view, O'Brien had reached very moderate conclusions about future Chartist tactics while in goal. Tired of violent talk about the need for physical force, which always petered out in ineffective argument, O'Brien decided that revolution by physical force was quite impracticable. Although Chartists should not co-operate with whigs or tories, they might well co-operate with middle-class reformers of good will, who had working-class interests at heart. For this reason O'Brien supported Joseph Sturge, the Birmingham Quaker, who in 1841 and 1842 created a Complete Suffrage Union to bring together middle-class and working-class reformers in support of a political programme which included both universal suffrage and repeal of the corn laws. When O'Connor opposed Sturge, O'Brien called O'Connor's policy 'Inconsistent, absurd and mischievous'. He was quickly dropped from the *Northern Star* team and was soon compelled to feel the weight of the invective which he had hitherto employed against others. He failed in his efforts to develop a rival Chartist paper pledged to 'no factious politics, but real democracy', and before long found himself being hooted by O'Connorites at local Chartist meetings. From 1844 to 1847 he lived in the Isle of Man, running an unstamped paper and fighting a propaganda battle against O'Connor.

O'Connor's attitude to middle-class co-operation was usually hostile, but he could be quite inconsistent, as most local Chartists were, in the kind of temporary alliances he was prepared to make. From 1843 onwards, however, he was primarily concerned not with the six points of the Charter as such, or how to secure them, but with his land plan, a scheme of settling industrial workers on peasant smallholdings bought and organised by a Chartist Co-operative Land Company. There was much that was Irish in his vision, and there was much in the vision that appealed immediately to the first generations of industrial workers. In the manufacturing towns, O'Connor claimed, people's lives were

embittered and shortened by excessive and ill-requited toil. In
the country they could find peace and independence. The
community as a whole would benefit too, he argued most
unrealistically, since smallholdings cultivated by spade husbandry
would produce more agricultural produce than the existing
large and small farms. Conditions in industry would improve
also as the new land settlements set a pattern of honest labour.
O'Brien thought that all this was nonsense. Peasant proprietorship was socially regressive and might destroy the whole basis
of radical politics. Moreover, in his view, the plan was a diver-
sion from more urgent political tasks, a sign of O'Connor's
megalomania, of his obsession with maintaining total power
over a mass movement. In reaching this conclusion O'Brien
was not very different in his views from William Lovett whom
he had once so much despised.

As recent writers have shown, O'Brien was not wholly fair to
O'Connor in his personal attacks and his criticisms of the land
plan. Yet the fairness or unfairness was politically immaterial.
O'Connor succeeded in retaining his hold on Chartism in the
eighteen-forties only at the expense of losing some of his most
able lieutenants. Increasingly he saw himself as the sole saviour
of his country, rejoicing, in his own words, that he was 'the
best abused man, not in England, but in the world'. When at
last he was returned to parliament in 1847 as member for
Nottingham, with a tory as a colleague, he could even claim
that it was a vindication of the policies he had advocated in 1841.

One year after O'Connor entered Parliament the revolution
which had been anticipated for so long at last broke out. It
broke out, however, not in England but in Europe. Against the
background of economic crisis, Chartism had its last
opportunity. A new petition was prepared, a new convention
was summoned, and a new wave of mass meetings in London
and the provinces was planned. There was no revolution.
Parliament showed no interest in the petition, the convention
was weak and divided and the mass meetings in London were
used as an excuse for a large-scale display of governmental
force. Only in the provinces was there large scale disturbance,
and there English and Irish grievances fused. O'Brien, a delegate
to the 1848 Convention as he had been to the Convention of
1839, now figured as a resolute opponent of all talk of physical
force. He was groaned off the platform when he told the delegates
that the government was too strong for them and that the
central Chartist leadership was out of touch with the people it
claimed to represent.

The following day O'Connor was involved in what has often
and usually misleadingly been called 'the fiasco of Kennington
Common'. Returning to the language of 1839 he had promised

that he would rather die than give up a particle of the Charter; 'our movement', he had said, is 'a labour movement, originated in the first instance by the fustian jackets, the blistered hands and the unshorn chins'. When it came to the point, however, he behaved in exactly the same way as O'Brien had talked. He agreed at once with the metropolitan commissioner of police that the petition had best not be taken to the house of commons, persuaded the crowd to disperse, and left for the home office in a cab. He is there said to have told Sir George Grey, the home secretary, 'the government have been quite right. I told the convention that if they had been the government they never would have allowed such a meeting.'.

Chartism did not die on Kennington Common, but by the end of the year it was clear that as a mass movement it had failed. By the end of another two years prosperity finally killed it off. O'Brien lived on until 1864, talking politics, writing politics and poetry, and quarrelling with people whose views he did not like. O'Connor's end was quicker, more dramatic, and more gloomy. He was never at his ease in the politics of the Chartist minority after 1848, politics of faction, when socialist Chartism 'Chartism with the red flag', was attracting the most able and energetic of the remaining leaders. His land plan was declared illegal and was wound up. He himself was removed from the house of commons in 1852 after being involved in an alarming scene with another member. He was pronounced insane and died in a private lunatic asylum in 1855.

The two men should be remembered not in their decline but in their prime. They quickened the pace of politics, and gave politics a genuine popular significance. They did many things and said many things which had never been done or said before. If the hopes which they held out were often far in advance of what could reasonably have been achieved at the time, then these were not days of reason in the English industrial areas, where their appeal was greatest. Against the background of a bleak age, both O'Connor and O'Brien added a sense of colour and purpose to many men's lives. Although they were exploiting hunger, they were also pleading for greater human dignity. Chartism had many elements in it, and no single moral. It is for this very reason that it still remains exciting, interesting and significant.

ASA BRIGGS.

JAMES FINTAN LALOR

In HISTORIES of Irish labour James Fintan Lalor has been accorded a position of great importance. He is seen as one of the great apostles of socialism in Ireland. In histories of the land question he is depicted as the prophet of Irish revolutionary land reform and he appears in political history as one of the evangelists of Irish nationalism. It is difficult to sort out the true character of the man who has been adopted by so many diverse leaders as their forerunner. Michael Davitt, Patrick Pearse and James Connolly all quoted Fintan Lalor freely and with approval and found in him a kindred spirit. In many ways, however, his views were not as simple as these political writers thought.

Lalor was almost forty years of age before he made a public appearance in the arena of politics. That was in a letter to Charles Gavan Duffy, editor of the *Nation* newspaper, in the beginning of 1847. We know little of his career before that time. He was the eldest son of Patt Lalor of Tenakill, near Abbeyleix, a prosperous tenant farmer, and was educated in Carlow Lay College for a couple of years, but had to leave because of ill-health which dogged his whole career. His father was a strong supporter of Daniel O'Connell in his struggle for Catholic emancipation, abolition of titles and repeal of the Act of Union. James Fintan at the early stage, parted company with his father's political views. While his father was a member of parliament from 1832 to 1834 James appears to have been influenced by a group of agrarian reformers in his native county. These were led by the erratic William Conner who put forward a scheme for arbitration on rents and fixity of tenure for tenant farmers. Conner's suggestions found few supporters but Fintan Lalor was one of them.

Conner held public meetings in various parts of Kildare and Laois and was ultimately charged with making a seditious speech at Mountmellick in 1841 for which he received a sentence of six months' imprisonment. Conner was later expelled from the Repeal Association because he proposed that repealers should pay no rent, county cess, rent charge, tithe poor rate or any other charge arising out of land until repeal was granted. James Fintan Lalor was intimately associated with Conner and spent weeks at his house near Athy. He also attended Conner's public meetings.

It was at this stage that his political differences with his father began. James realised that the fundamental problem in Irish rural society at that time was the system of land tenure. Daniel O'Connell maintained that land reform would follow the setting up of an Irish parliament. He agreed that reform was needed but that it should follow the repeal of the Act of Union. In this view he was supported by Patt Lalor.

Looking around at the social condition of the Irish rural population Fintan Lalor chafed at such delays. He saw that the people were living at a level little removed from starvation. There were, in 1841, over eight million people in the country. At least one half of them were living at bare subsistence level. There was an acute struggle to make a living on microscopic holdings. With high rents and small farms, a very large proportion indeed being less than ten acres, many tenant farmers were as badly off as day labourers who were paid fourpence to sixpence a day with diet or eightpence to a shilling a day without diet. The labourer had no security, however, since he had no guarantee of employment. The small farmer had at least a foothold on subsistence while he retained possession of his land.

The pressure of population however, meant more and more competition for land and higher rents. The social system gave landlords almost arbitary powers of ejectment and the tenant farmers had no security of tenure. Lalor saw the danger of more and more of them being evicted and forced to join the already overcrowded ranks of day labourers. This was the situation when he decided, in the summer of 1843, to make a direct appeal to the prime minister, Sir Robert Peel. The repeal movement was at its height but Lalor was not satisfied that it would help the people to improve their condition. He wrote to Peel:

> I have long seen and felt . . . the absolute necessity which exists that *all* agitation for political objects should entirely cease before any improvement can be effected in the condition of the Irish people. I am most anxious that the present repeal movement should be speedily and safely suppressed not imperfectly and for a period, but fully and forever.

He went on to admit:

> I was myself at one time something more than a mere Repealer in private feeling—but Mr. O'Connell, his agitators and his series of wretched agitations first disgusted me into a conservative in point of feeling; and reflection and experience have convicted me into one in point of principle.

While we have not got Lalor's complete correspondence with Peel it appears to be clear that he hoped to convince the Prime Minister that he could suppress the repeal movement if he, at the same time, adopted Lalor's plans for a settlement of the land question. Peel was obviously impressed and submitted one of Lalor's letters both to the home secretary, Sir James Graham, and to Prince Albert. It is possible that the government's decision to follow the banning of the Clontarf repeal meeting and the prosecution of O'Connell with a commission of enquiry into the land question was influenced by Lalor.

In the meantime, however, James Fintan had retired again into obscurity. Apparently his differences with his father forced him to leave his home at Tenakill and he lived precariously for some time in Dublin and Belfast. A severe recurrence of his long-standing tuberculosis resulted in a reconciliation with his father in 1846 and he returned home. Events of this period again brought him forward in politics. The famine was crucial in driving him to take up the pen once more on behalf of the tenant farmers. The lives and land of the tenants were more insecure than ever. Peel had failed him. The commission of enquiry had reported but the government had taken no action. The severest shock to Lalor's conservatism was probably Peel's sudden conversion to free trade. The repeal of the corn laws threatened to reduce the prices which Irish tenant farmers might receive for their corn crops and so make it more difficult for them to pay their rents and to support themselves. The defeat of Peel's administration on a coercion bill for Ireland in the summer of 1846 ended Lalor's hopes from the conservatives.

Political events were taking place in Ireland at the same time which gave Lalor some hope. The Young Irelanders in the Repeal Association broke with O'Connell and walked out of the organization. Some months were to pass before the seceders set up an association of their own, but Lalor took a keen interest in them and followed the columns of the *Nation*, eagerly looking for expressions of their views. The young men, Gavan Duffy, Thomas Francis Meagher, Thomas D'Arcy McGee, John Mitchel and Michael Doheny, seemed to hold out a new hope to Lalor. When they decided to found the Irish Confederation in January 1847 Lalor wrote to Gavan Duffy. Here, at last, was an Irish movement independent of O'Connell and, in fact, opposed to his leadership.

Lalor had, by now, cast off the shreds of his conservatism. Influenced by the nationalism of the Young Irelanders he developed his theories on social and political questions. He now became a republican and in the columns of the *Nation* he was given space to publish his views. He set out principles governing private property which fitted in with his newly found republicanism. He maintained that the origin of private property lay in a social contract. He wrote:

> When the independent families who form the natural population of a country compose and organise into a regular community, the imperfect compact or agreement by which each man holds his land must necessarily assume the more perfect shape of a positive and precise grant from the people . . . That grant must necessarily assume and establish the general and common right of all the people as joint and co-equal proprietors of all the land.

While this reasoning would seem to lead to the total abolition of private property such was not Lalor's aim at all. His aim was to provide a theoretic basis which would protect the rights of tenants and limit the absolute rights of property as then exercised by landlords. He applied principles of English legal theory to the Irish situation. In England the ultimate ownership of the land rested in the crown. In a republican Ireland Lalor substituted 'the people' for 'the crown.' According to him the people could give grants of land to landlords exactly as the crown had done with but one modification; the people, as original owners, would not give the landlords power to oppress themselves as tenants. 'No man,' wrote Lalor, 'has a right to hold one foot of Irish soil otherwise than by grant of tenancy and free from them, and under such conditions as they may annex of suit and service, faith and fealty'. In this Lalor was basing his limitations on the property rights of landlords not on distributive justice, but on his own interpretation of the eighteenth century social contract theory.

Lalor set out his objects and aims in telling letters:
> Our fair share of Ireland, our fair share of the earth, a house to live in that no one can tumble down, a happy home, the necessaries of life, the comforts and decencies of life, all those things without which the world is worthless and existence itself a misery: these we must have and security for all these.

This was his principal object and he maintained that it was of greater interest and importance to the people than repeal of the Union. Just as he had proposed to Peel that he weaken the repeal agitation by doing something to solve the land question now he tried to link the national and economic questions together so as to strengthen both.

In his letters Lalor made it clear that his work was on behalf of the small tenant farmer and not the agricultural labourer.

He wrote:

> In every district the tenantry are being evicted in
> hundreds. . . . These men are being converted into 'in-
> dependent labourers'; and the number already evicted will
> form a very considerable addition to a class too numerous
> even now for the demands or resources of the country—
> too many to be absorbed—too many to be supported.

He included, however, among his small farmers the agricultural labourers who had even a small allotment of potato
ground. Of these he said :

> Each man had at least a foothold of existence . . . The
> lowest grade of these men were miserable enough; but not
> so utterly so as the mere labourer. Their country had hope
> for them too, while she had none for the labourer.

The condition of the independent labourer he considered to
be beyond repair. His aim was to prevent more and more people
being reduced to their ranks.

During the spring and early summer of 1847 Lalor appealed
on behalf of the smallholders in the columns of the *Nation* and in
letters to Duffy, McGee and Mitchel. Duffy was willing to allow
him to appeal to the landlords through the paper but was not
satisfied to allow him to push through a clear-cut policy. Lalor
had decided that, if the landlords continued to clear estates, the
one answer was for tenants to refuse to pay rents. In this he
got no support in the Irish Confederation. Despairing of any
active help from that body he went to Tipperary in the summer
of 1847 and, with the aid of Michael Doheny, founded a tenant-
right league. Again, however, he found it impossible to bring
about a strike against paying rent and, disappointed, he returned
to Tenakill.

The events of the following year were exciting. Mitchel
broke from Gavan Duffy and set up a more vigorous newspaper, the *United Irishman*. He wrote to Lalor to win his aid and
admitted that he had been wrong in not supporting him the
previous summer. However satisfying it may have been to
Fintan Lalor to have his policy get a belated benediction from
Mitchel, he was still too annoyed over the earlier failure to
co-operate with him. The temper of politics in the early months
of 1848, however, grew hotter. The revolution in Paris had an
immediate influence on Young Ireland. Mitchel became more
and more violent and, in May was arrested, tried and transported
on a charge of treason felony.

John Martin, Mitchel's brother-in-law, decided to carry on
Mitchel's policy in a successor to the *United Irishman*. This was

the *Irish Felon*, and he enlisted Fintan Lalor's aid in editing it. Lalor moved to Dublin and, for the first time, made personal contact with the Young Irelanders.

He was caught up in the enthusiasm and feeling which the extradition of Mitchel had aroused. He threw himself zealously and feverishly into politics. He hoped that the *Felon* office would be 'an armed post, a fortress for freedom . . . never to surrender nor stoop its flag until that flag shall float above a liberated nation.'

To those who had read his forceful letters his personal appearance came as a surprise. He was small, delicate-looking and hunch backed but his fiery enthusiasm soon impressed them. He set about organising Felon Clubs with members throughout Ireland and even in England. Among those who corresponded with Lalor and became a founder of a Felon Club in Staleybridge in England was a well-known Chartist, B. T. Treanor. Lalor wrote regularly for the *Irish Felon* but his writings were directed more to exciting an insurrection than to social questions. He did, however, show his interest in movements such as Chartism. When John Martin was arrested early in July he proposed a scheme for a newspaper which might succeed the *Irish Felon* if it were suppressed. Among his suggestions he said that one at least of its editors should be an English Chartist of known talent and honesty.

The course of events in Dublin at this time, however, kept Lalor fully active in trying to bring out the *Irish Felon* regularly after Martin's arrest. In the issue of July 15, it was announced:

> The members of the 'Felon Club' must excuse us for not attending to their communications this week. Our office arrangements have been somewhat disturbed by the burglarious attacks of her Majesty's licensed plunderers. Some of our papers were seized—which is about the most unpleasant part of the affair. They were 'felonious' enough, at all events.

For three weeks he brought out the paper before a date was set for the rising. On July 22 he ended his last article.

> Somewhere, and somehow, and by somebody, a beginning must be made. Who strikes the first blow for Ireland? Who draws first blood for Ireland? Who wins a wreath that will be green for ever?

The government had suspended the Habeas Corpus Act and the Young Irelanders who were still at liberty had to act quickly or allow themselves to be arrested as Martin, Duffy, D'Alton

Williams and O'Dogherty had been in the preceding weeks. They chose to scatter and organise risings at various points. Smith O'Brien, Meagher and a number of others ended up at Ballingarry. Lalor went to north Tipperary. McGee was sent to Glasgow to rouse the Irish there. Lalor visited Borrisoleigh and was arrested at Templederry before he had organised any action. He was lodged in jail by the time the abortive struggle took place at Ballingarry.

Lalor spent several months in Newgate prison before being released in November of that year. His health had deteriorated and it was thought that death was imminent. However, after his release, he gradually recovered and, even during his convalescence, carried on feverishly with plans for organising another rising. He gathered round him a number of young men whom he inspired with his own indomitable enthusiasm. Lalor wrote to Gavan Duffy at this time: 'There is a very general fermentation going on below the surface. The movement everywhere is running spontaneously into secret organization and I think natural tendency ought to be aided, not interfered with.'

In fact secret organizations in south Tipperary and Waterford had been organized by Philip Gray and a similar body was set up in Dublin. In the city the secret organization depended largely on democratic labour groups. The members included John O'Leary, Thomas Clarke Luby, Charles Kickham and many others who later became well-known Fenians. Lalor was at the centre of these as was his former colleague from the *Irish Felon*, Joseph Brennan, who was now editor of the *Irishman*.

His closest association, however, was with Luby. The latter had heard many stories of Lalor's ill-temper and irritability. Nevertheless he found in Lalor a pleasant and congenial friend. Lalor, Luby and Edward Keatings were elected as an executive committee of the organisation but there were a number of disputes. Fintan Lalor was anxious to establish a new newspaper to succeed the *Irish Felon* and Brennan, as editor of the *Irishman*, was not anxious to have any competition. Brennan had supporters within the society and sought to oust Lalor. When the latter left Dublin to visit Father John Kenyon in Templederry in the early summer of 1849 Brennan took over leadership in the city.

During his visit to the country Lalor spread the society in County Tipperary and Limerick. He called a public meeting in Limerick city in support of his newspaper project. In the meantime, in Dublin, Lalor's opponents in the society were pressing for a rising and did actually plan to kidnap Queen Victoria during her Irish visit in August 1849. This was a fiasco but did not end the schemes for a rising. Early in September a meeting of Dublin and country members of the society was held in Clonmel. It was decided that on Sunday, September 16, simultaneous risings should take place in Cork, Limerick, Clare, Kilkenny, Tipperary and Waterford.

The society was united in this project but the numbers expected did not turn out for the rising. At Cappoquin alone, was any action taken. There the police barracks was attacked by a party led by Brennan. Two policemen were killed but the attackers were driven off. Lalor lay out all night waiting to lead an attack on Cashel barracks but he was joined by a force which he considered totally inadequate. He dismissed them towards daybreak and dispiritedly returned to Dublin.

He considered joining the staff of the *Nation* which Gavan Duffy had revived. His spirits and enthusiasm soon returned, however, and once more he pushed forward with his plans for establishing his own newspaper. Again his health declined, this time irreparably, and he died two days after Christmas, 1849. His influence remained. The young men who had acted with him in his last year were to carry into the next generation the plan of organization which was the basis of Fenianism. Lalor's writings, however, lay neglected in the files of the *Irish Felon* and of the *Nation*. The only available collection of them was among the extracts produced as evidence in the trial of John Martin in 1848. Among Fenians, especially in America, Lalor's name was not forgotten but it was an opponent of the Land League, P. H. Bagenal, who revived an active interest in his writings. Bagenal in his anxiety to gain some obscure political advantage tried to prove that the Land League's policies originated with Lalor. In his publications he quoted freely from Lalor.

From 1896 onwards an easily accessible edition of Lalor's writings was available and James Connolly and other Labour Leaders took a great interest in them. Connolly himself prepared a pamphlet containing selections from them and they were frequently quoted in socialist circles. Peadar Macken wrote in the *Irish Nation* in 1910: 'Lalor, if not a socialist in the modern sense, was at least convinced of the truth of the socialist doctrine in so far as it related to a country mainly, if not entirely, agricultural.'

This interpretation of Lalor is also to be seen in Connolly's *Labour in Irish history* and, in the light of many of Lalor's statements, there might appear to be just grounds for it. However, a closer analysis of Lalor's writings bears out the view that he was not a socialist but that he had the interest of all workers at heart. His political programme, however, was aimed at the protection of the tenants who held some land no matter how small.

Pearse wrote before the Rising in 1916: 'Tone sounded the

gallant reveille of democracy in Ireland. The man who gave it
its battle-cries was James Fintan Lalor.'

These battle-cries have not always been interpreted in the
same way. Pearse's understanding of Lalor was possibly better
than Connolly's because Pearse was a lawyer who understood
the legal terminology which Lalor used. This did not prevent
the writings of Lalor being the basis of rapprochement between
the two leaders in 1916 and in the proclamation of the republic
the thoughts of Lalor are incorporated. R. M. Henry has written
that Pearse's last pamphlet, *The sovereign people*, was an attempt
to establish on the basis of the writings of James Fintan Lalor
the thesis that the independence claimed for Ireland was both
republican and democratic. There is little doubt that it was
upon the basis of some such understanding that Pearse's
followers and those of Connolly joined forces and that Lalor
played no small part in Labour's contribution to 1916.

In the struggle which followed Lalor's writings continued to
play a part.

While the 1916 prisoners were still in jail a selection from
Lalor's letters to the *Nation* and the *Felon* newspapers was
printed, only to be followed by a more complete edition the
following year. This edition carried a preface by Arthur Griffith
and one can find the shadow of Lalor in the negotiations which
led to the sending of a delegation to London in 1921. Lalor had
stated a principle in 1848: 'In order to negotiate the parties must
stand on equal terms and each be independent of each other'.
That principle was just one of the stumbling blocks in Irish
politics forty years ago and it shows the survival of the influence
of James Fintan Lalor down to the very end of the fight for
Irish independence.

THOMAS P. O'NEILL.

MICHAEL DAVITT

AMONG THE Irishmen who played a notable part in the rise of
the labour movement in these islands, Michael Davitt (born
1846, died 1906) holds a unique place. He was already established
in the imagination of his countrymen as the 'father of the Land
League', and as a national leader was second only to Parnell
when he threw himself into labour politics. He remained a
leading and active nationalist, and retained the confidence and
affection of the Irish masses, but after 1882 much of his time and
energy was given to the labour movement and given mainly in
Britain. For he identified the stuggle of British workingmen for
political emancipation and social justice with the peasant revolt
in Ireland that he had inspired and led. He came to believe that
national independence could only be won for Ireland with the
support of the British working classes; and despite discourage-
ment and the open opposition of Parnell himself, he persevered
for the rest of his life in his self-appointed task of teaching the
working-classes of both countries to understand each other's
problems and of advancing the labour movement in Britain.
He took some part in promoting labour organisation in Ireland,
but it was a minor activity. For the conditions that had enabled
him to lead the forces of social revolution in Ireland in the days
of the Land League were not repeated. After 1882 Britain offered
a more promising field for his political genius, and he had no
doubt that, in working for the victory of industrial democracy
in Britain, he was serving the cause of the common man in
Ireland as well as the cause of national independence.

The peculiarity of Davitt's position as a labour leader reflects
his personality. He was a man of high courage, moral no less
than physical, warm-hearted and passionate, intolerant of
cruelty and injustice, of large sympathies and quick perceptions,
strong-minded, and self-reliant almost to the point of fanaticism.
It was seldom that he was not fighting for some cause that he
believed to be just or for some individual or group that he
regarded as the victim of injustice. He was a man of ideas, and
was inclined to see political issues in abstract terms, yet he was
no doctrinaire; for he was so conscious of human suffering and
so anxious to be of service to his fellow men that he was prepared
to work for objectives that fell far short of his ideals. A rugged
individualist, his characteristic role after 1882 was that of a
political free-lance. He was frequently involved in fierce public

controversy and was ready to defend his views against any opponent, however formidable; and yet, for the sake of some public advantage, he would sometimes draw back, or yield to the judgment of others. Partly this was because, though impulsive, he was diffident and self-critical; but partly also because, though a born independent he accepted the democratic principle, holding that the minority must be prepared to submit to the majority while endeavouring to win acceptance for its own views. Though often disappointed and despondent, he preserved a sober optimism and a robust faith in the common man. He read widely, had cultivated tastes, and was a gifted writer—from 1877 he earned his living mainly by journalism. Yet he was largely self-educated, and was in the strictest sense a man of the people, being the son of an evicted peasant who had fled with his young family from county Mayo to the Lancashire cotton-town of Haslingden. There, at the age of nine, Davitt was working twelve hours a day in a cotton mill, and he was just over eleven when he lost his right arm, through a machine accident. The accident ended his factory career and nearly ended his life. Then two years of unexpected schooling opened the way to more congenial employment with the local postmaster. His early kinship with factory workers was one of the formative influences in Davitt's life; another was the experience of mixing with people of a different religion from his own. An Irish catholic in the midst of English protestants, he grew up free from religious animosities, and learnt very young to deplore the folly of working men who allowed sectarian bigotry to obscure their common interests.

Davitt graduated to the first rank of Irish nationalism through five years' service in the secret revolutionary organization, the Irish Republican (or Fenian) Brotherhood, followed by seven years in penal servitude. He emerged from Dartmoor on ticket-of-leave in 1877 to become an architect of a 'new departure' in Irish politics. The exciting new tactics of Parnell in the house of commons were infusing a fighting spirit into the home-rule movement at the same time that an accumulation of rural distress in Ireland was bringing on an agrarian crisis unparalleled since the great famine. Davitt, through the formation of the Land League in 1879 under Parnell's presidency, coupled the home-rule movement to a great popular agitation for a radical settlement of the land question. Nationalists of all shades of opinion joined the Land League, thus forming a popular front to which the most militant element was contributed by Fenians, won over by Davitt's example from secret to open action. The resulting 'land war' (1879–81) was the greatest mass-movement of nineteenth-century Ireland. Technically legal, it was animated by the spirit of social revolution, and Gladstone's government met its challenge by a combination of coercion and concession. By the end of 1881 it seemed that the league was beaten; but in fact it had won a decisive battle against Irish landlordism and given a decisive impulse to the advance of democracy in Ireland.

The spirit and methods of the Land League were those of trade unionism on the offensive, and Davitt was eager to emphasise its universal implications. 'The principles upon which this land movement rests are founded upon . . . natural justice. . . . The cause of Ireland today is that of humanity and labour throughout the world.' To convince the workers of Britain that the struggle of the Irish peasants was also their struggle seemed highly important to him, but his hands were too full to take up the task before he was rearrested and sent back to prison in February 1881. Fifteen months under relatively lenient conditions in Portland gave him ample opportunity for reflection on the land question and other social problems, and laid the foundations of his first book, *Leaves from a prison diary* (completed in 1884, published in 1885). Here he formulated a theory of land nationalization that linked the cause of the Irish peasantry with the cause of labour in general.

The battle-cry of the Land League—'the land of Ireland for the people of Ireland'—meant only one thing to the tenant farmers, their transformation into owners of their holdings, and this was in fact what the land war eventually brought about. Davitt had hitherto not clarified his ideas on the subject, and in the thick of the fight had been content to concentrate his energies on the overthrow of the landlords. Now he propounded a doctrine of national ownership of the land that combined his own ideas with the teaching of Henry George, whose famous book, *Progress and poverty*, had appeared in 1879. Land was a unique commodity: it was no man's creation, it was essential to all life, and it was fixed in quantity. It ought therefore to be directly owned and administered by the state. Private monopoly in land meant that the landlord appropriated most of the wealth produced by labour, returning only a bare living to the tenant. Under national ownership the tenant would enjoy the full product of his industry and would have a virtual freehold in his farm, paying a tax equal to the annual value of the bare land and observing certain conditions: the holding must be cultivated, it must not be sub-divided beyond specified limits, it should not be larger than the tenant could personally manage, and the state should have the right to authorise mines and minerals to be worked in it, subject to reasonable compensation. Comparing this scheme with peasant proprietorship, Davitt argued that the mere multiplication of landowners through state-aided land-purchase would not remove the evils inherent in the private ownership of land, and in particular that it would benefit neither the agricultural labourers nor the industrial workers. Under national ownership, on the other hand, both these classes would share in the new prosperity of the farmers through the liberation of land now lying waste or idle, the abolition of all taxes save the single tax on land, and the elimination of speculative land values. Now however defective were the economics of this scheme, it was of enormous importance in Davitt's thinking as a remedy for the wrongs of the working classes as a whole; and to it Davitt adhered in principle for the rest of his life. Though he was never a socialist in the ordinary sense, this basic agrarian theory tended always to impel him into the socialist camp.

In *Leaves from a prison diary* Davitt also appears as a pioneer in the theory of labour representation in parliament. Despite the extension of the franchise since 1832, government in Britain was still virtually the monopoly of privilege and wealth, and from this fact flowed social injustice, imperialism, and war. The remedy lay in the exercise by the workers themselves of functions now blindly delegated to their employers. If workers would organise for electoral purposes, they 'could return a labour party fifty or sixty strong to the house of commons, instructed to act independently of political parties and with a view to the interests of labour. To facilitate this vital change the workers should demand that election expenses be made a charge on the rates and that salaries be provided for M.P.s. The advent of an independent labour party would challenge the supremacy of wealth, now entrenched in the house of commons, and would put an end to that stronghold of privilege, the house of lords.

Davitt was thus more extreme in his views than ever when he emerged from Portland in May 1882 to find that he owed his release to a compact between Parnell and Gladstone—the 'Kilmainham treaty'—whereby Gladstone agreed to improve upon his land act of 1881 while Parnell agreed to damp down the land agitation and co-operate with the liberals in restoring order to Ireland. To Davitt this compact seemed a disaster: Parnell, he considered, had surrendered the Land League for a small concession at a time when English rule in Ireland was more shaken and demoralised than it had been since 1798, and when, therefore, by keeping the agitation going, he might have won not only better terms for the tenants but also a measure of home rule itself. The Kilmainham treaty was the vital turning-point in Parnell's career, and he turned in the wrong direction: from having been a revolutionary reformer he became an opportunist statesman. Though this view of the Kilmainham policy proved to be true in the sense that Parnell thereafter firmly held the national movement on a constitutional course, Davitt continued to support Parnell's leadership while insisting on the right to advance the national cause in his own way. He wanted to revive the land agitation and to direct it to the goal of nationalization; to link the cause of the agricultural labourers and the urban workers with that of the tenant farmers; to identify the Irish national movement with the aspirations of the British working classes and to make the Irish party the champion of their interests in parliament. He began to campaign on these issues in 1882, and during the next few years carried on a vigorous propaganda for land nationalization and the policy of a labour alliance, working outwards from the areas in which the Irish element was strongest—Lancashire, Yorkshire, Tyneside, the Clyde and the London area—and becoming one of the best known platform figures among the Irish leaders.

These activities drew down a resounding rebuke from Parnell on 15 April 1884. What could be more preposterous than to expect the Irish peasant to renounce the goal, now almost within sight, of occupying ownership, and adopt the new craze of land nationalization? And as to Davitt's labour alliance, 'we are told', said Parnell, 'of some great wave of English democracy which is coming over here to poor Ireland to assist the Irish democracy. The poor Irish democracy will have, I fear, to rely upon themselves in the future as they have had to do up to the present.' It is probable that at this point Davitt could have started a dangerous recession movement and would probably have received strong American-Irish backing for it. He decided instead, in the interests of national unity, to swallow his pride and keep silent. In the following year he reacted strongly against Parnell's decision to instruct the Irish in Great Britain to vote for conservatives in the general election of 1885, when the greatly enlarged electorate provided for by the reform acts of 1884–5 would be brought into action for the first time. To Davitt such tactics were as repugnant as the Kilmainham treaty: the conservatives were essentially the party of privilege, of vested interests, of imperialism; as between the two great parties the only hope for Ireland lay with the friends of democracy, the liberals. The conservatives soon proved that the hopes they had raised were illusory; and Gladstone's conversion to home rule in 1886 brought Parnell and Davitt together again.

Convinced of Gladstone's integrity, and moved by his splendid audacity, Davitt wholeheartedly supported the policy of the liberal alliance, which from 1886 onwards was the official policy of the home rule party. But he lost none of his interest in working-class politics, and, as a current began to set in favour of the plan of independent labour action that he himself had been foremost in advocating, his sense of obligation to the liberals came into conflict with his labour outlook. While he inclined increasingly to the left, he felt impelled to argue that a 'lib.-lab.' policy was, for the time being, the most sensible for labour. Yet the mounting urgency of the social problem was plain to him. He was the principal speaker at the Easter Monday labour demonstration in Hyde Park in 1887. The conflict inherent in lib.-lab.ism was brought home to him by the Mid-Lanark by-election in 1888. The contest marked the first attempt of James Keir Hardie, formerly a miner, now secretary of the Scottish Miners' Federation, to contest a seat in parliament; and as he was an advocate of an independent labour party, though still a liberal, the election was regarded as a test case. It was the more interesting to Davitt because there was a strong Irish element in the constituency. Hardie was willing to stand as an official liberal candidate, but was looked upon by the party's central office as too extreme, and therefore likely to cause a stampede among the timid, monied element in Gladstone's following. For the same reason Parnell, despite Davitt's efforts, was unwilling to give Hardie the support of the Irish party. Hardie then declared himself an independent labour candidate, and as a result had to fight both the liberal and the home-rule parties. Yet his programme included home rule for Ireland and in his argument for a separate labour party he actually invoked the example of Parnell and the Irish party. Davitt joined with Scottish labour leaders in campaigning for Hardie, but Hardie was heavily defeated by a liberal in a three-cornered fight.

From 1888 onwards Hardie and other labour leaders, fired by socialist idealism without being dogmatic socialists, denounced the labour alliance with Gladstonian liberalism as a fraud, and insisted that labour could not fight for its rights effectively unless it treated liberals and conservatives alike as enemies. This policy took practical shape in the formation of the Scottish Labour Party in 1888 and, still more decisively, in that of the Independent Labour Party, under Hardie's chairmanship in 1893. The I.L.P. was one of the main roots of the present British Labour Party, formed in 1906. The Labour Party was the realization of one of Davitt's own ideas, and if Davitt had not felt himself committed, as a nationalist, to the liberal alliance he might well have become a partner with Hardie and his friends in founding it. Instead, his adherence to a lib.-lab. policy brought about an estrangement from Hardie that lasted for many years.

If, as Davitt believed, the time was not yet ripe in Britain for independent labour representation in parliament, it was still less so in Ireland; and this made it all the more urgent that the Irish parliamentary party should be in the vanguard of social reform. But under Parnell's conservative leadership the party was in fact lagging behind the liberals. Davitt was specially concerned about the condition of the agricultural labourers and other unorganised workers, and in an effort to defend their interests he helped to found at Cork, in January 1890, the Irish Democratic Trade and Labour Federation. He then suggested to the president and secretary of the Dublin Trades Council that a conference of trade unionists should be held in Dublin to discuss the formation of a general labour federation for Ireland. Such a conference met in 1891 and led to the foundation, three years later, of an Irish Trade Union Congress, on the model of the British T.U.C. Davitt's attempt to put reformist pressure on the Irish party elicited barbed criticism from Parnell: 'What is trade unionism but a landlordism of labour? I would not tolerate, if I were head of a government, such bodies as trade unions. . . . Whatever has to be done for the protection of the working-classes . . . should be the duty of the government. . . . You are overlooking Mr Gladstone's . . . difficulties. . . . Your new labour organization at Cork will frighten the capitalist liberals and lead them to believe that a parliament in Dublin might be used for the purpose of furthering some kind of Irish socialism.'

Though far from unmindful of Gladstone's difficulties Davitt next embarked on the adventure—long contemplated—of a penny weekly newspaper, the *Labour World*, 'a journal of progress for the masses'. Produced and published in London and intended for popular consumption throughout the British Isles and beyond, it made a remarkably good start in September 1890. Press comments were friendly and over 60,000 copies of the first issue were ordered. Though it had much to say about Irish affairs it was not addressed primarily to Irish readers, and its main emphasis was on labour interests. While taking an independent line in politics and by no means tender towards liberal shortcomings, it was lib.-lab. rather than socialist in sympathy. Well produced, competently written, and covering a wide range, it had no rival in its own particular field. But Davitt was temperamentally unfitted to the grind of a newspaper office, and after four months his health broke down. He had staff difficulties from the start, and his printers gave him ironical experience of the tyranny of trade unionism! The capital that a few English supporters raised for him proved insufficient. In less than eight months he resigned the editorship and the paper collapsed.

In the disruption that followed the O'Shea divorce, Davitt flung himself with characteristic ardour into the struggle against Parnell, whom he regarded as morally discredited and therefore intolerable as leader. He worked hard to build a strong national party out of the majority who repudiated Parnell, and after Parnell's death he successfully contested a seat in parliament—much against the grain. His entry into parliament in the general

election of 1892 coincided with the return of the liberals to
office under Gladstone, pledged to a second attempt to carry
home rule. More deeply committed to the liberal alliance than
ever, Davitt used his influence in the majority party to re-
commend labour men as nationalist candidates for seven Irish
constituencies. Two of his nominees, Michael Austin and
Eugene Crean, returned in 1892, were the first labour-nationalists
in the party. Keir Hardie entered parliament at the same time
as an independent labour member, at war with the liberals. To
Davitt, Hardie and his friends now seemed an arrogant and
unscrupulous faction, dangerous to the interests alike of labour
and of home rule. This remained his attitude till the end of the
century, despite the fact that Hardie voted with the liberals for
the second home-rule bill (1893). The killing of that measure
by the house of lords only intensified Davitt's attachment to the
liberals, to whom he looked for the abolition of that 'den of
land thieves'.

Davitt was wrong about Hardie but so also was Hardie about
Davitt. He regarded Davitt's conduct towards Parnell in the
divorce crisis as an unscrupulous and malicious attack on the
one man who had proved himself capable of leading the Irish
nation out from the morass of party politics on to the firm rock
of national independence. In 1897, in his famous manifesto,
Young men in a hurry, he coupled Davitt with Bradlaugh and
Burns as men who could have led the democracy of Britain
whither they would but who had succombed to the seductions
of the liberal party and thus lost their terrors for the oppressors
of the people. But Davitt was far from being the extinct volcano
of Hardie's imagination, as his dramatic stand against the Boer
war—involving his withdrawal in disgust from parliament—
abundantly showed. He became increasingly disappointed with
the liberals after Gladstone's retirement. In 1900, the reunion
of the Parnellites with the main body of the nationalists on the
one hand, and a broadening of the basis of I.L.P. policy through
the setting up of the Labour Representation Committee on the
other, helped to remove misunderstanding between him and
Hardie. Their reconciliation was complete by 1905, when they
agreed on a policy of co-operation between nationalists and
labour in the next general election.

As a result of this agreement Davitt took a prominent part in
the general election of 1906, campaigning on behalf of labour
candidates in the London area, the midlands, South Wales,
Lancashire and Yorkshire. He took up an advanced labour
position, without committing himself to socialism, and combined
this with advocacy of home rule. Against the efforts of the
catholic hierarchy in England and Ireland to make the education
question a vital issue wherever the Irish vote was involved, he

bluntly contended that, in general, schools supported out of public funds ought to be undenominational and that the particular question of catholic schools in England was not a vital issue in the election. For this attitude he was fiercely assailed after the election by the catholic bishop of Limerick and the catholic archbishop of Dublin, and he was battling in the press with both prelates when he was struck down by the illness that proved fatal on 30 May 1906; but not before he had the satisfaction of taking part in the great demonstration in the Queen's Hall, London, with which the new Labour Party celebrated its electoral victory: it had run 50 candidates and had returned 29 as compared with 2 in the preceding general election.

It is as hard to assess Davitt's achievement as it is impossible to doubt the greatness of his influence. He saw none of his ideals fully realised. He has an assured place in Irish history for his leadership of the peasantry in the land war, but the eventual outcome of the struggle, peasant proprietorship, was not the solution of the land problem at which he aimed. He dreamed of a solution, national ownership, that would reanimate the national life of Ireland by benefiting the whole working population. But his championship of nationalization found little response in Ireland and made converts chiefly in Britain. Two other self-appointed tasks engaged much of his energies during his last 25 years: furthering the labour movement and teaching the working classes of Britain and Ireland to co-operate. What success he attained in these unfinished endeavours is uncertain, but I am convinced that his contribution to the history of the British labour movement was considerably greater than has yet been recognised. His strength lay, I think, in the influence of his personality on ordinary men throughout Ireland and Britain and beyond. Ordinary men who came in contact with him had no doubt of his sincerity, his integrity, his courage, and his compassion. In Britain he became a symbol of the international solidarity of labour. In Ireland he was probably the best loved and most trusted of all the nationalist chiefs of his day. As Keir Hardie put it: 'Ireland's cause was no mere political banner to him. His Ireland was the actual, flesh and blood Ireland—the poor and the oppressed'. And W. P. Ryan has well said of him: 'His grand unspoiled soul is not to be measured by the actual programme that in difficult days he found feasible. His influence on the spirit of the workers was uplifting and energising. They felt his power and began to feel their own.' Yet it would be wrong to suppose that his greatness rested on service to a class interest as such. For he served his fellow-men under the impulsion not of any dogma but of a generous and compassionate spirit that surmounted all distinctions of class and circumstances no less than of religion and national origin.

T. W. Moody.

WILLIAM WALKER

WILLIAM WALKER is probably the least well-known of Irish labour leaders. Yet he had such a following in his own day that he nearly won a seat in the British house of commons as the first labour M.P. from Ireland. If he had been successful he might even have swung Irish trade unionists into the British political labour movement. As it was, he held up the formation of an Irish Labour Party for ten years, and he set a pattern to be followed by the labour movement in Belfast, his native city.

In the early eighteen-nineties Belfast's public forum, familiarly known as the 'steps', was its near Palladian custom house and surrounding square. Here every Sunday afternoon when the weather permitted crowds would gather to be edified, amused or even infuriated. There were no women among them, though there might be a few boys mitching from Sunday school, and all would be wearing the Sunday-best clothes of the working class. The speakers—most of them lay preachers of some kind, either individuals or members of evangelical bodies—had their regular pitches. Two groups were noticeably different. There was always a large crowd gathered around Arthur Trew, who for some years carried on a one-man crusade against the evils of popery and of ritualism in high places, larding his speeches with Biblical texts and jokes in doubtful taste. The second group was that gathered round the Belfast branch of the young Independent Labour Party.

The I.L.P.'s principal spokesman was William Walker, then a young man in his early twenties. He was of medium height, wore his hair long and affected a bohemian tie and a soft black hat. A fluent and aggressive speaker, with plenty of energy and self-confidence, he was most effective when attacking local corruption. Possible slander actions did not deter him, for in those days public men were less sensitive than they are to-day. He was also quite ready to speak on the usual I.L.P. topics. If he dealt in generalities, as when he was describing the socialist society of the future, he would quote with special relish St. Paul's saying: 'He that shall not work, neither shall he eat.' He loved words of learned length and thundering sound: once when he was deploring the divisions in the Irish labour movement he declared: 'In the alembic of a Divine mysteria it is hard to reason the whys and wherefores of our conflicting opinions.'

But I have introduced the young Walker without giving his background, and as he cannot be understood without it I must describe the city in which he grew up. Not the Belfast of our day, which Walker would scarcely recognise, except perhaps on the 'Twelfth', but the city as it was in his youth, towards the close of the last century.

Walker was born over ninety years ago, in 1870. Belfast was smaller than Dublin then, but it was growing so rapidly that it doubled its population by the end of the century and caught up with the capital. Many of its 350,000 inhabitants were rural labourers and small farmers who had deserted the land for the industrial and commercial capital of Ireland, as its citizens liked to call Belfast. It had shipbuilding, engineering and textile industries—and a good deal of the ugliness that went with manufacturing in those days. It had its quota of jerrybuilding, as a public health inquiry showed in 1896. One site a speculator wanted to build on was so bad that the chairman of the inquiry described it as an enormous dunghill. A third of the houses had dry privies, many streets had no back access and pigs could be kept fifteen feet from a dwelling-house. Some of the worst evils, however, were swept away within ten years and the mean rows of kitchen houses never sank into the condition of squalor and overcrowding that made the tall tenements of Dublin notorious. A workman paid a lower rent and had a better chance of getting and keeping a job than elsewhere in Ireland. One lord mayor of Belfast pointed out these facts to a congress of the Irish T.U.C. in 1898 and declared that as a result Belfast was 'an elysium for the working man.'

The skilled worker in heavy industry might not agree that his existence was idyllic, but at least he could live comfortably on his wages of £2 a week or more if he remained in constant employment. Shipbuilding in the yards of Harland and Wolff and Workman, Clark gave work to well over 10,000 men; it was, however, a dangerous occupation and accidents accounted for half of the industrial fatalities in Ulster. But the general labourer and especially women, children and juveniles in the linen trade paid heavily in terms of low wages and wretched working conditions for the industrial greatness of their city. Factory inspectors' reports make grim reading. Occupational diseases and accidents killed or crippled many; an 1893 report stated that on an average seventeen years of work killed a carder. Poverty drove large numbers of married women, widows and children into spinning mills and weaving factories. Where no paid leave was given pregnant women might work until birth pangs began and return to the mill a few days after their delivery.

Juveniles suffered as well as their parents; in 1906 the Belfast death-rate for the fifteen-to-twenty age group was twice that of Manchester, which had its own unhealthy cotton industry. Then there were the half-timers, children of school age who earned as little as 2s. 9d. for a fifty-six-hour fortnight. Their plight was summed up by a spinner who pointed out a group to a woman factory inspector and said, 'Ah! indeed they're hard enough wrought.' Half-timing was not abolished until 1920.

A great deal of the making-up work for the linen trade—shirts, handkerchiefs and bed-linen—was done outside the factory in the home. Over half of the women outworkers in Belfast could earn no more than a penny an hour, and in some cases employers reduced their earnings still further by charging them more than the cost price of thread. Factory inspectors did their best, but they were few in number. After repeated demands by Walker and his comrades in the Belfast Trades Council and the Irish T.U.C. more were appointed, but when they did prosecute, local magistrates who sympathised with the employers refused to convict or inflicted fines of a few pence. In this respect Ulster had perhaps the worst reputation of any factory district in the British Isles.

Sweated industries were not the only serpents in the working-man's Garden of Eden. Perhaps the most venemous was the politico-sectarian feeling which grew stronger in the last quarter of the nineteenth century. The working class was sharply divided on catholic-nationalist and protestant-unionist lines. Few catholics belonged to the skilled trades in heavy industry. The two sections also lived in different districts; the Falls road, for instance, was nationalist, the Shankill road unionist. In times of tension the minority in an area were liable to be driven out of their homes and even their jobs. Trouble could easily break about July 12, the date of the annual orange 'walk'. (Nationalist processions were fewer and less important.) The 'Twelfth' demonstration was a colourful sight. Thousands of brethren in sober black suits, bowler hats and orange regalia marched in lodge formation to the chosen field to hear the orations of their leaders. Each lodge had its own banner commemorating King William or some local orange hero, and was accompanied if possible by a flute band or great 'Lambegs', the enormous drums which produced a sound like heavy gunfire and had an intoxicating effect on sympathisers. But the brave pagentry might end in police charges when fighting broke out on the borders of a nationalist district. If a home rule bill was being debated clashes were inevitable and the cobbled streets of those days supplied plenty of ammunition. The first great riot in Walker's lifetime occurred during the home rule debates of 1886, when he was still in his teens. Twenty-nine lives were lost.

Walker began his working life as an apprentice joiner in Harland and Wolff's shipyard. He also began trade union work there, for he helped to organise some of the semi-skilled men, the platers' helpers, before he was out of his time. His own union, the Amalgamated Society of Carpenters and Joiners, soon recognised his ability and appointed him as a delegate to the Belfast Trades Council, the leading body of its kind in Ireland. Its members were staid, conservative tradesmen who prided themselves on their respectability and importance in the community. They were deeply offended at not being asked to present in person their loyal address of welcome to a visiting lord lieutenant. When Keir Hardie held an Independent Labour Party meeting in Belfast they warned 'the working men of the city to take no notice of irresponsible parties who are endeavouring to propound their ideas under the mantle of trade unionism and labour.' They disliked Walker's politics but they could not deny his energy and ability. As a result he was appointed temporary secretary of the Textile Operatives' Society of Ireland, a union for the sweated women linen workers, and so met such leading British trade unionists as Hardie and Ben Tillett. He was one of the Belfast delegates to the first congress of the Irish T.U.C. in 1894 and was chosen to reply to the toast 'The Labour Cause' at the congress banquet.

Within a few years Walker had conquered his opponents in the council and was elected secretary. In the short run it was a doubtful honour, for it led to his being dismissed by the firm in which he worked—he had written to the British war office complaining that the firm was not observing the fair wages clause in its contract. He was blacklisted in Belfast and had to depend for support on the trades council, which paid him 23s. 6d. a week victimization money for some months from its meagre funds. In the long run he gained rather than lost by his dismissal, for when the position fell vacant in 1901 his union elected him as a full-time official. Craft unions do not as a rule make permanent appointments and Walker had to come up for re-election every three years. There are cases where an official may have to go back to the bench after years of service but Walker had no such difficulty in that way, for his members were only too glad to retain him until his resignation.

Walker was now the official of a powerful British union and a dominant figure in the labour movement of his city. In January 1904 he was elected to the Belfast corporation where he led the labour group. He enjoyed municipal politics and had a keen nose and a vitriolic tongue for corruption. His principal target was the lord mayor, Sir Daniel Dixon, who had begun life in the timber trade, but had made a fortune in building contracts and land speculation. In one deal he sold some sloblands to the corporation, and, though he claimed the price was a fair one, Walker wrote an article attacking him mercilessly. The headlines will give a very fair idea of what it was like, they were: 'AT IT AGAIN—ROBBING THE RATEPAYERS—DODGER DAN'S DEAL'. On this occasion Dixon did take an action for libel and won it.

The picture I have given you earlier may have left you with the impression that Belfast was a backward town, but, in fact, it was well ahead of other Irish towns in a number of ways. The corporation supplied gas and electricity at cheap rates, water for many years had been a public enterprise and the transport system was taken over as soon as the existing leases permitted. No other town had done as much. Labour in Belfast gave a lead too; the first Irish parliamentary labour candidate fought a seat there as early as 1885, thirty years before one appeared in Dublin. He was Alexander Bowman, a flaxdresser who had founded the city's trades council and fought the north Belfast seat on very little money. Though he was defeated he polled a respectable vote for those days. Twenty years later Walker, the second Irish labour candidate, also fought the same seat.

In the meantime circumstance had changed for the better from a labour point of view. Home rule was not a burning issue as the British conservative government was trying to kill it with kindness instead of coercion. Trade union organization was stronger and Walker had persuaded the unions to form a branch of the Labour Representation Committee, the fore-runner of the British Labour Party. His own union had put him on their panel of parliamentary candidates and was prepared to pay his election expenses and, if he were elected, a parliamentary salary as well. The Irish T.U.C. were hopeful that their former president's 'ringing voice would be heard ere long in the house of commons demanding equality and justice for the workers of his native land.'

Walker had prepared carefully for the coming general election, setting up labour clubs in the division to act as ginger groups. The contest, however, came a little sooner than he had expected, for the sitting member died and a by-election took place in September 1905. It was a straight fight against his old enemy, Sir Daniel Dixon, though perhaps 'straight' is not quite the appropriate word.

Walker's election machinery worked well and he had an expert election agent in Ramsay MacDonald, who had come over to assist him. Robert McClung in his manuscript reminiscences tells of his own experiences as a canvasser. The response was excellent. There were, of course, occasional electors whom nothing could shake—the man who said he would support an ass if his party put one up, the elector who declared he was going to vote for King Billy. Bowman in the earlier fight had adopted an equivocal attitude to home rule, in fact he was a supporter of Gladstone's Irish policy. Walker made no bones about declaring that he was 'a Unionist in politics', as well as a labour candidate.

Such a statement represented his real convictions and appealed to unionist electors. It did not seriously imperil the 1,000 nationalists votes on the register, votes which normally went to an anti-unionist candidate. At this stage the Belfast Protestant Association intervened. Arthur Trew had started it in the eighteen-nineties and with it had made I.L.P. meetings impossible. Walker himself had narrowly escaped with his life in one attack and had been given police protection for a year. But in the meantime Trew had been displaced by T. H. Sloan, a shipyard worker, familiarly known as 'Tod'. Sloan, who had been elected as an independent unionist candidate for south Belfast in 1902, and had also started the Independent Orange Order when he was suspended by the official body. This is not the place to pursue the fascinating history of the Independents or the efforts of their Grand Master, Lindsay Crawford, to have them follow his own evolution towards a liberal nationalism. It is sufficient to say that the Belfast Protestant Association was still in existence and that its secretary, Richard Braithwaite, attempted to make Walker and Sir Daniel Dixon give replies to thirteen questions supplied by the Imperial Protestant Federation. Braithwaite was kept at bay by Dixon's agent, but he had better luck with Walker. He cornered him one night when he was alone and presented him with the questions. Walker, hard pressed and fearful of losing votes, answered them. He committed himself to the retention of the British sovereign's accession declaration against transubstantiation, which described the 'sacrifice of the Mass' as 'superstitious and idolatrous', and to the exclusion of catholics from the offices of lord high chancellor and lord lieutenant of Ireland. When asked if he would place the interests of protestantism before those of the political party to which he belonged he made the remarkable reply: 'Protestantism means protesting against superstition, hence true protestantism is synonymous with labour.'

Walker's election committee were badly shaken when they heard what he had done, and Ramsay MacDonald wanted to resign, but was persuaded to carry on. Sir Daniel Dixon refused to answer the B.P.A. questions, the nationalist vote was split, and with the aid of an army of paid canvassers and hundreds of vehicles he won narrowly; his majority was less than 500 in a total poll of over 8,000.

At the general election a few months later Walker fought Dixon again, and was again defeated, though he managed to

increase his own vote and cut down his opponent's majority to
300. A year later Sir Daniel died and Walker, whose wife had
died some months earlier, very reluctantly agreed to stand again.
But the tide had turned and this time he was beaten by nearly
2,000. Walker made no further attempt to win an Irish seat.

In one sense Walker quitted Irish political life in 1907. He
made several attempts to recover the corporation seat he had
lost, but they were less and less the campaigns to be expected
from a labour representative. His last effort was an individual
one; he described himself as 'The People's Candidate' and did
not mention his endorsement by labour bodies. The truth was
that he had shifted his interests to British politics. He was
several times a member of the British Labour Party executive
and contested, unsuccessfully, the Scottish seat of Leith Burghs
in 1910.

Walker left the labour movement for good when he accepted
a post in 1912 as a representative of the newly established
national insurance commissioners. Some of his supporters felt
that they had been deserted, others, and there is some evidence
to support them, argued that Walker intended to return to
politics after the new social services, in which he was keenly
interested, had been well established. As it turned out he held
his post for only a few years. After a long illness he died at the
end of 1918, while still in his forties.

It is worth while attempting an estimate of Walker's qualities
and his contribution to the Irish labour movement. He was an
effective public speaker, inspiring his followers with his own
enthusiasm and at times winning over unsympathetic or hostile
audiences. He, more than any other man, made it possible for
the tender plant of labour representation to take root, if not to
flourish, in the ungrateful soil of Belfast during the opening
years of this century. He was undoubtedly, for a short period,
the most prominent figure, if not the leader, of the Irish labour
movement. He had little capacity, however, for self-criticism;
in a period when there were no outstanding men in the Irish
labour movement he was too conscious of his ability to suffer
opposition lightly, or treat it as other than personal disloyalty.
Along with the ruthlessness he occasionally displayed in inter-
union disputes went a certain weakness, best shown in his
yielding to B.P.A. pressure. And his rhetoric was too grandiose
to have any lasting effect, it became vague, even meaningless at
times and never contained the striking phrases that make
Larkin's still worth reading.

As a political thinker Walker was unoriginal. Too much of
what he wrote is concerned with long-dead local problems.
His powers of analysis were weak and when he generalised he
became verbose. His one positive contribution to labour

thought in Ireland was his policy on what used to be called
'The Irish Question'. In 1908 he gave a public lecture on that
subject and later had it published as a pamphlet. In it he argued
that the establishment of an Irish parliament would be a retro-
grade step, for it would bring no social or economic benefit
which could not be better obtained from a British parliament.
'Ireland a nation' for him implied no more claim to separate
statehood than 'Scotland a nation'. The socialist creed was
internationalist, not nationalist. He recognised local differences,
which could be met by the granting of greater powers to local
authorities—in other words he was an advocate of 'gas-and-
water' socialism.

Not long after Connolly returned from America Larkin
appointed him organiser in Belfast for the Irish Transport and
General Workers' Union. Walker and Connolly soon clashed.
Belfast delegates to Irish T.U.C. congresses had always opposed
attempts to form an Irish Federation of Trade Unions or an
Irish Labour Party. In 1911 Connolly wrote to the Glasgow
Forward, pleading for a merger between his Socialist Party of
Ireland and the Belfast branches of the I.L.P. Home rule was
inevitable, united action was necessary and the Irish T.U.C.
should form an Irish Labour Party. Connolly, however, did not
limit himself to such suggestions, he criticised Walker strongly
for his unionist declarations in the north Belfast elections.
Walker replied and after six articles the controversy was closed
by the editor.

Neither of the contestants emerged with much credit from the
ill-tempered, indeed abusive debate. Connolly claimed that his
party had a true conception of internationalism, 'a free federation
of free peoples', while the Belfast I.L.P.'s conception was
'scarcely distinguishable from imperialism, the merging of
subjugated peoples in the political system of their conquerors.'
Defending the Belfast I.L.P., Walker asserted that owing to its
work no religious riot could take place in the city, a statement
disproved a year later by the Castledawson troubles. Walker's
pride in Belfast's municipally owned services and his super-
ficial remarks about Irish history drew from Connolly the retort
that the real objection in Belfast to Irish socialist unity was
based on parochialism, not internationalism.

Connolly's charge was not without justification, yet it is not
a complete explanation of Walker's attitude. Caught between the
hostile and sectarian-ridden forces of nationalism and unionism,
Belfast labour leaders had little room for manoeuvre. Frustrated
at home, they turned east for deliverance. This hope is clearly
expressed in Walker's last article in *Forward:*

> I am an internationalist because the same grievances
> which affect the German and Englishman affect me. I speak

the same tongue as the Englishman; I study the same literature: I am oppressed by the same financial power, and to me, only a combined and unified attack, without geographical consideration, can assure to Ireland an equal measure of social advancement as that which the larger and more advanced democracy of Great Britain are pressing for.

Walker failed in his objective to merge the Irish in the British labour movement, though it is interesting to speculate on what might have happened had he won a seat in 1905. In the year after the *Forward* debate, when Walker was no longer in politics, Belfast delegates such as D. R. Campbell and T. R. Johnson helped to carry at the Irish T.U.C. a motion forming an Irish Labour Party. Yet Walker's aims were dictated by his environment, and since that environment has as yet undergone no radical change, they still command support. But, more than half a century after Walker's struggles his political heirs have found these aims no easier of fulfilment.

J. W. BOYLE.

JAMES CONNOLLY

JAMES CONNOLLY was the faithful and fervid historian of many of the leaders and workers with which this series of broadcasts deals. In *Labour in Irish history*, and elsewhere, he popularized Lalor, he brushed the dust off Philosopher Thompson's writings, he revived the memory of the social and political impact of Irish pioneers on Great Britain and the United States: of Feargus O'Connor, James Bronterre O'Brien, John Doherty, and Devin Reilly. He made controversy to some purpose with William Walker, and history to even greater purpose with Jim Larkin, and, James Connolly, after many dedicated years to the labour movement in Great Britain, America, and Ireland, then passed himself into history in Easter Week, 1916, with the question: 'It has been a full life, and isn't this a fitting end?'

Unfortunately, however fitting the end, Connolly within a few years was buried in a shroud of words, both by his enemies and by his friends. Therefore, those to-day who never knew him in his lifetime must turn to his powerful and persuasive writings, and discover (if they can) the message, personality, and spell of a man from the world of nearly fifty years ago.

And even then, James Connolly was a man who belonged to, and worked in two worlds: the world of international socialism and the world of militant nationalism. He told his daughter, Nora, that John Mitchel's *Jail journal* had been his Bible in his boyhood, and, according to family tradition, he spent many an hour with an uncle who was a Fenian. John Leslie, the man who later turned Connolly into a socialist, introduced Connolly to a second Bible in the writings of Karl Marx. Very early, his bitter father's stories of the hard lot of the workers, and his own bitter experiences kindled his unquenchable hatred of social injustice.

From the two enthusiasms for Mitchel and Marx came the uniqueness of James Connolly in his time, and the labour leader of 1913, and the leader of the 1916 insurrection, as unique as the land owner William Thompson of Cork in the twenties of the nineteenth century or of Fintan Lalor in the forties, three men who made history and whose words made history not only in Ireland but far beyond her shores.

Of the three men, Connolly alone had direct and first-hand experience of black and grinding poverty. The phases of that life are known in outline. He was born in Edinburgh on

5 June 1868 of Irish parents. His mother was a Monaghan woman, and Connolly always claimed with pride 'I am a Northman myself'. His boyhood in the Scottish city was a hard one, spent in blind-alley jobs, in a bakery, in a printing office, and in a tiling factory. His latest biographer, C. Desmond Greaves, has established through Connolly's correspondence and other evidence, that this phase was rounded off by some years of service in the British army—whether in Ireland or abroad is still uncertain. This experience was reflected in Connolly's first writings in some of the most vitriolic anti-militarist outbursts he ever wrote. Even if this experience gave him a military training, and, more than most socialist writers of his time, an acute awareness of the reality of military force, his personal loathing of those years flares up relentlessly more than once. As, for example, in the 'Soldiers of the Queen' article in the *Workers' Republic*, 15 July 1899, on the eve of the South African war:

> The demoralising effect of this occupation is further exemplified in the life and language of the soldier himself. . . . The army is a veritable moral cesspool corrupting all within its bounds . . . a miasma of pestilence upon every spot so unfortunate as to be cursed by its presence.

In 1889 Connolly abruptly quitted the army some months before his service had expired, and returned to Scotland. Possibly the news of a severe accident to his father who was employed in the cleansing department of Edinburgh Corporation hastened his return. He was 21. After his marriage to Miss Lillie Reynolds at Perth on April 13, he settled in Edinburgh, and worked as a carter for the Corporation. These were the years when the socialist and labour movements and militant trade unionism were gathering force in Great Britain. The Social Democratic Federation with William Morris, H. M. Hyndman, Tom Mann and others were conducting a vigorous campaign. Connolly attended some of their meetings. He was won over by John Leslie, a Co. Waterford man who had been secretary of a Ribbon lodge in his youth, a poet and hard-hitting speaker. The influence of Leslie's pamphlet, *The present position of the Irish question*, first published in the nineties in the Social Democratic Federation paper, *Justice*, is very plain in Connolly's earlier writings. The Fenians, and the Land League above all, are held up as the most democratic and real of Irish movements. The old sympathetic link between the United Irishmen and Scottish reformers, and between Young Ireland and the Chartists in the forties is emphasized. Leslie did something more for Connolly: he turned him into an orator after

Connolly by sheer will power had mastered a serious impediment in his speech. Some words he never did conquer, socialism for example, which to the end for him was 'soc . . . iysm.'

In 1894 Connolly stood as a socialist candidate for the Edinburgh Town Council. He was defeated after a campaign long remembered in the city. He met Keir Hardie and his colleagues who had founded the Independent Labour Party the year before. Connolly came to regard that organization as a far more effective model of what a popular movement should be than the Social Democratic Federation. Hardie's biographer, William Stewart, has described the Connolly of those days:

> James Connolly . . . a most unCeltic-like personality, slow and difficult of utterance, yet undeterred by any disability of physique or training from delivering his message, a very encyclopedia of statistical facts and figures and of Marxian economics, a victimized industrial martyr even then, but with nothing either in his demeanour or in his political views foreshadowing his tragic and heroic end at the head of an Irish rebellion.

Some years later in Dublin, one of Connolly's colleagues of those days, Bruce Glasier, however, had a strong hint of what those political views really were when he saw Connolly heading a stormy popular demonstration against the Boer war, waving the Boer flag, calling for the defeat of Britain in the Transvaal, and cheering in that spring of 1900 for an Irish republic.

After the Edinburgh election Connolly certainly was an industrial martyr. He had resigned his job with the corporation, an experiment with a cobbler's shop failed, and he could not find employment anywhere. At last, he made full arrangements to emigrate to Chili. His wife and Leslie protested strongly. Then Leslie acted on his own.

As Edinburgh correspondent of the Social Democratic paper, *Justice*, he wrote bitterly in December 1895 that he must make public the plight of James Connolly, an unskilled labourer with a wife and small family, one of the ablest and most intrepid propagandists the labour movement in Scotland had turned out,—destitute through his services to the movement, and with difficulty induced to defer his intention of emigrating.

Leslie's appeal concluded:

> Is there no one in Glasgow, Dundee or anywhere who could secure a situation for one of the best and most self-sacrificing men in the movement . . . an unskilled labourer —a life-long total abstainer, sound in wind and limb (. . . how often have I nearly burst a blood vessel as those

questions were asked of myself?) married with a very young family; and, as his necessities are therefore very great, he may be had cheap.

An answer came which changed the course of Connolly's life nor was it the last time that emigration was to change it significantly. Leslie and Connolly had followed eagerly the Land League and Parnell struggles, and as eagerly the repercussions of the great London dock strike on trade unionism in 1889, the year of Connolly's return to Scotland—repercussions which had affected Ireland as well as Great Britain. In Ireland many branches of the Gas Workers' Union had been established and an eight hours day secured for gas workers in Irish towns. Keir Hardie's Independent Labour Party had one branch in Dublin which carried on an active propaganda. Its work was somewhat hampered by the lack of literature relating the struggle to Irish conditions, and by criticisms that it was an 'English' organization. Its members differed in outlook, from that of those future colleagues of Connolly, Tom and Murtagh Lyng, who leaned towards the marxism of the Social Democratic Federation, to those like Robert Dorman of Ulster—later Senator Dorman, Northern Ireland—who followed Keir Hardie with the New Testament rather than Marx's *Capital* for their text book. To meet the objection that the organization was a 'foreign' one the name was changed to 'The Dublin Socialist Society.' When Leslie's appeal was published in *Justice*, the society invited Connolly to Dublin as their organising secretary. He agreed and arrived in the city with his family in May 1896.

On Connolly's advice the Dublin Socialist Society was dissolved and the Irish Socialist Republican Party formed on 29 May 1896. A manifesto was issued, the first paragraph of which sums up Connolly's lifelong policy:

> The struggle for Irish freedom has two aspects: it is national and it is social. Its national ideal can never be realized until Ireland stands forth before the world a nation free and independent. It is social and economic, because no matter what the form of government may be, as long as one class owns as private property the land and instruments of labour from which all mankind derive their substance, that class will always have power to plunder and enslave the remainder of their fellow-creatures. . . . The party which would lead the Irish people from bondage to freedom must then recognise both aspects of the long-continued struggle of the Irish nation.

Two years later, on August 13, 1898, the *Workers' Republic* appeared under Connolly's editorship, backed with a £50 loan by Keir Hardie, always a close personal friend. They differed in their views on socialist doctrine and tactics often. Yet Connolly's moving obituary of Hardie in October 1915, and his praise of Hardie's aid to the Dublin workers in 1913, and his tribute to Hardie's stand against the first world war show the essential bond of spirit between them, and one of the passions that drove him to his own death in the Easter Rising: 'Keir Hardie stood resolutely for peace and brotherhood—refusing to sanction the claims of the capitalist class of any nation to be the voice of the best interest of that nation.'

That August of 1898 Connolly in his paper defined what he understood by a workers' republic: 'A socialist republic', he wrote, 'is the application to agriculture and industry, to the farm, the field, the workshop, of the democratic principle, of the republican ideal.' His first two pamphlets, *The new evangel* and *Erin's hope*, elaborated this. The *Workers' Republic* had, of course, to be produced by the voluntary labour of his party members. Some crusty trade unionists denounced them as blacklegs until Connolly descended on the Dublin Typographical Association with the devastating question: 'When we shave, do we blackleg on barbers?'

Connolly's propaganda made little impression on the separatist groups which had arisen after the centenary celebrations of the 1798 insurrection, although his relations with them were friendly. He wrote for Alice Milligan's *Shan Van Vocht*, debated at the Celtic Literary Society where he met Arthur Griffith, William Rooney, Pearse and W. B. Yeats. He and his party took part in the tumultuous anti-jubilee protest of 1897 and in the anti-Boer war meetings in 1900. The Irish Socialist Republican party contested without success five municipal elections in Dublin. Twice Connolly stood for the Wood Quay Ward, backed by the Dublin Trades Council, on which he at one time represented the United Labourers' Union. In 1903 during Connolly's second contest, Arthur Griffith wrote in the United Irishman: 'We are not socialists, but we would be intensely gratified to see a man of Mr. Connolly's character returned to the Dublin Corporation to let the light in on the corruption that sits enthroned on Cork Hill.'

Behind all this was waged Connolly's unending battle with hardship and poverty. When he first came to Dublin he worked as a labourer on the main drainage scheme, later as a proof reader on a Sunday newspaper, as shipyard worker, builders' labourer, pedlar, and at other casual jobs. His salary as party organiser of a pound a week was sporadic. Yet through all this insecurity and penury, with his family in a one-room tenement, Connolly read widely and deeply with an unquenchable thirst for history, for economics, and poetry. Once a member of his party belittled Byron for his erring ways. Connolly retorted that they had nothing to do with Byron's quality as a poet, and moreover, Byron had cursed the Georges and fought for the Greeks.

From 1902 onwards Connolly was in close touch with the Scottish branches of the Social Democratic Federation which had come under the influence of the American Socialist Labour Party, and its leader Daniel De Leon with his syndicalist or industrial unionist theories. Connolly adopted and adapted these theories; his *Socialism made easy* is his best and clearest exposition of this.

Finally in 1903 Connolly decided to emigrate with his family to the United States. The hard pressure of his exacting struggle to live, some personal differences on policy with his colleagues, and a preliminary lecture tour the previous year for the American Socialist Labour Party, which had published an edition of *Erin's hope* with a preface by De Leon, all helped in his decision. He thought he had seen Ireland for the last time, and little knew the lessons America was to teach him.

Some vivid flashes of Connolly during his seven years' stay in the United States are given by Elizabeth Gurley Flynn, who worked with him in the Irish Socialist Federation and the Industrial Workers of the World, in her autobiography, *I speak my own piece*. She met him first at an out-door demonstration in Washington Park, New Jersey, where he worked in the Singer Sewing Machine Factory, a job which he lost when he tried to organize a union in the plant.

Her impression of him was somewhat sombre, 'dark sad eyes, a man who rarely smiled', somewhat hampered when he spoke to American audiences by his 'thick North of Ireland accent, with a Scotch burr from his long residence in Scotland.' Once they attended a meeting of Italian socialists. She and Connolly spoke first and an Italian speaker was announced for after the interval. During the interval the Italians gave the two speakers coffee and cakes instead of the stale water they were given at most meetings. For once Connolly smiled when she asked him who would speak in Italian, and merely said. 'We'll see. Some one surely.' Then Connolly himself took the platform, and made a short speech in Italian to the loud applause of the delighted audience.

In some detail Elizabeth Gurley Flynn describes Connolly's stormy and varied career as organiser for the Industrial Workers of the World, his final break with the rigid doctrinaires of the Socialist Labour Party and De Leon, his later lecturing tours for the more liberal Socialist Party of America, his founding of the Irish Socialist Federation, and his monthly paper, *The Harp*. She notes, and her experience of the American and internationa labour movement was as wide and exciting as his own, 'Connolly was the first person I ever heard use the expression, "Workers' Republic", none of us had ever heard the word in those days.'

As for the *Harp:* 'It was a pathetic sight to see him standing, poorly clad, at the door of the Cooper Union, or some other East Side hall, selling his little paper. None of the prosperous professional Irish, who shouted their admiration for him after his death, lent him a helping hand at that time.'

Her last picture of Connolly is his leavetaking of the Flynn family just before his return to Ireland:

'The baby was very fretful that day. Connolly, who was well experienced with babies, having had seven, took the baby from me, laid him face down across the knees, and patted his back until he went to sleep.'

His life in the United States, though more easy than his earlier life in Scotland and Ireland, was as mixed in its occupations. Apart from his union and lecturing activities, which took him on long train journeys all over the American continent, he worked in turn as a linotype operator, machinist, insurance agent, and manager. He wrote to his old friend and colleague, William O'Brien—the man later responsible for preserving and publishing most of his more important writings—that though he was always dreaming of Ireland and his return home, 'I could not go into the Dublin slums again to live; one experience of that is enough for a lifetime.'

At the invitation of a small Dublin committee, of which William O'Brien was organizer and secretary, Connolly returned to Dublin in June 1910 to lecture to the Socialist Party of Ireland, then newly revived on a broader basis than the old organization's. On his return, his old friends congratulated him on his improved appearance, and he drily retorted, 'while I was away, I got something to eat.' Yet America had done more than that for him. He had matured as a thinker, speaker and writer. De Leon had cured him once and for all of the old rigid doctrinaire argumentation, even if the influence of Marx swayed his thought to the end. His slogan now was, 'Less theorizing and more fighting'.

The closing paragraph of his programme for the new socialist party appealed to 'all workers, and to all honest friends of progress in any rank of life' to rally to his party and the 'gathering working class movement' for one great objective—'the common ownership of the means of producing and distributing all wealth . . . common ownership of our common country, the material basis of the higher intellectual and moral development of the future.'

Then on the eve of the years of action, Connolly published in 1910, *Labour in Irish history*, his interpretation of the position of labour in the great epochs of Irish history, and the attitude of political leaders to social justice, In *Labour, nationality, and religion*, his brilliant polemic against Father Kane's anti-socialist Lenten sermons, he repeated his consistent case that socialism was exclusively a political and economic question. The infuriated De Leon, six years before, had called Connolly 'a Jesuit agent' for saying the same thing.

In July 1911, Connolly became secretary and Ulster district organizer of the Irish Transport and General Workers' Union, and settled in Belfast. From then on, two outstanding leaders dominated the Labour movement, Jim Larkin and James Connolly, an uneasy yet loyal alliance, described by a friendly critic as the alliance of the tornado and the light house.

As Connolly turned to organize the mill girls and dockers of Belfast or the Wexford foundry workers a year later, he hammered home a new message: 'In building up the Union we are raising Ireland up!' His was the first voice raised in warning against the first hints of political partition and its menace to the future of the labour movement. Against the sectarianism of the A.O.H. and the Orange Order he raised the slogan: 'I don't care where a man worships; but I do care where he gets his pay on a Saturday night. I don't care where a man worships, but I do care that he has a man's rights allowed to him, and that he is a man standing along with his fellows in the common battle for the uplifting of the human race.' At the Irish Trade Union Congress in Clonmel (May 1912) he made a rousing speech in the debate which led to the formation of an independent labour party, for the then expected home rule parliament.

All his trials and triumphs prepared him for his two last great battles. Through all the eight months' chronicle of the Dublin strike of 1913 with its violence, hunger, endurance; with some twenty thousand workers standing out against a powerful combination of employers for the elementary right to belong to what union they chose; through every phase of what he summed up as a 'drawn battle'. Connolly survived many exacting tests; whether in his daily leadership in Dublin: in Mountjoy jail on hunger-strike; in the memorable orations at the popular demonstrations he addressed in Great Britain or at tense debates at trade union conferences there; in his writings in the *Irish Worker* and *Forward* which preserve a living and detailed record of the impassioned agony of the wearing struggle; in the eventual disillusion when defeat stared him in the face with the refusal of the British trade union leaders to go beyond moral and financial support.

Through it all Connolly lived through some of the finest and greatest hours of his life, of which few short and crowded years remained. With the outbreak of the first world war, he realised that the crisis of his life and his ideals was upon him, that long awaited Day of Wrath of which he is a prophet throughout all his pages, what a line in one his poems calls, 'The crowning point of history, the child of bitterest need', in a word, his long waited revolution. The outbreak of the war in Europe, the collapse of the international socialist movement, and, final stroke, Redmond's speech committing Ireland to the war, shook him to the depths. From then on, James Connolly became the active propagandist, and one of the driving forces towards insurrection. 'We believe that in times of peace we should work along the lines of peace to strengthen the nation, and we believe that whatever strengthens the working class strengthens the nation. But we also believe that in times of war we should act as in war,' runs one passage in the article in his *Workers' Republic* on 22 January 1916, in his best testament, 'What is our programme?' And all Connolly is there, with something of the ring of Mitchel and Lalor in the words.

'Nothing could break the will of this man' said the doctor who attended him, as he lay a wounded, half-dying man, staring out at the fires of O'Connell Street, and refusing to be moved from his leadership and the post of danger.

DESMOND RYAN.

JIM LARKIN

WHEN JIM LARKIN came to Dublin in 1908 he was thirty-two
years of age—a handsome young man, tall and broad-shouldered,
with a commanding presence. His hat was dark and wide-
brimmed—and my mother remembers it being rumoured in
those early days that he never removed it, because he was
anti-Christ and was obliged to hide a third eye that was set in
the centre of his forehead.

Indeed, many terrible things had been said about him already.
During the Belfast labour troubles of the previous year, for
instance, the press, having warned its readers on different
occasions that he was either a socialist, an anarchist, or a
syndicalist, decided to make the case against him as black as
possible by labelling him a papist. Very soon the press in Dublin,
with a similar desire to suit its revelations to its audience, was
referring to him as an orangeman. Later it decided he was an
atheist. When this failed to dislodge him from the esteem of his
devoted 'rabble of carters and dockers,' a photograph of Larkin
appeared in one newspaper side by side with a drawing of Carey,
the informer. In the caption above the photographs the question
was put to the readers: 'Is Larkin the son of Carey?' So it will be
seen right away that, had Larkin been so endowed, a third eye
would have been a comparatively minor handicap.

As it happened, Jim Larkin, born in 1876, was the second
son of improverished Irish parents who had emigrated to
Liverpool, and he had spent nearly all of the first five years of
his childhood with his grandparents in Newry. It was a very
brief childhood. At the age of nine he was back in Liverpool, a
breadwinner now, working forty hours a week for a wage of
2s. 6d.—plus a penny bun and a glass of milk which his employer
gave him every weekend as a sort of bonus. Later, he went to
sea and sailed to South America; then, on his return to Liverpool
he became a foreman on the docks, until he lost his job through
coming out in sympathy with the men under him. This action
of his—the first blow in a fight which was to last his lifetime-led
to a position as temporary organiser for the National Union of
Dockers.

The appointment proved very temporary indeed. Jim Larkin's
militant methods during the Belfast disputes of 1907 alarmed

not only the employers, but the executive of the union he served. James Sexton, the general secretary, said of him:

> Jim Larkin crashed upon the public with the devastating roar of a volcano exploding without even a preliminary wisp of smoke. I have myself been called an agitator and have not resented it. Believe me, however, in my earliest and hottest days of agitating I was more frigid than a frozen millpond in comparison with Larkin. . . . I was feeble, tongue-tied, almost dumb.

And, what was worse in James Sexton's eyes, Larkin proved himself quite unamenable to discipline. In Belfast his new weapons of the sympathetic strike, his doctrine of tainted goods and his wildfire oratory closed down job after job with alarming inevitability. He persuaded the members of the police force who were supposed to be keeping the strikers in order that they were underpaid for this difficult and unpopular work—and it ended with the police going on strike too. Belfast became an armed camp, with soldiers bivouacking in the streets. All this was far too fast and furious for the Liverpool executive. Alarmed at the turn events had taken, they took matters out of his hands altogether by excluding him from the negotiations and the ultimate settlement.

Larkin was not a man either then or at any point throughout a stormy lifetime, to submit to being overruled by others. Besides, the conservative outlook of the accepted trade unionism of the time did not appeal to him. Already, he had plans in mind for the formation of an Irish based union which would make full use of the new revolutionary techniques under his own control and leadership. And already, in the imaginations of the more timorous, he was the Visitation with the Third Eye.

Dublin, in 1908, provided as disturbing a picture as any revolutionary might look on. In order to see the events of those early years in proper perspective, let us spend a little time examining that society, through some official records that have been left for us. At that time the population of the city, which then excluded Pembroke, Rathmines and Rathgar, was 305,000 people, of whom 87,000 (or about one third) lived under quite terrible conditions. These destitute 87,000 people occupied the cast-off houses of the rich and they walked about—for the most part—in the cast-off clothes of the middle classes. D. A. Chart in a lecture delivered about this time, gives us a picture of children and old people searching the bins of the well-to-do for cinders; so that even the fuel of the poor, or a substantial part of it, was gathered through the same casting-off process.

The tenement houses were divided by the housing inquiry of 1913, in its official report, into three categories:

Those which appeared structurally sound; those so decayed as to be on the borderline of being unfit for human habitation and those unfit for human habitation and incapable of being rendered fit for human habitation.

The structurally sound houses accommodated 27,000 persons; the borderline houses 37,500; while 23,000 people lived in the tenements which the commission had declared to be absolutely unfit for habitation. In other words, one third of the population lived under conditions injurious to physique and morality.

So much for the houses. Now let us look at the living conditions by examining some typical evidence given at the enquiry. One witness described seeing a room sixteen feet square occupied by the two parents and their seven children. They slept on the floor, on which, according to the witness, there was not enough straw to accommodate a cat and no covering of any kind whatever. The children were poorly clad; one wrapped in a rag of a kind, and his only other clothing a very dirty loin cloth. Furniture? Nothing. A zinc bucket, a can, a few mugs or jampots for drinking. Rent—2s. 3d. weekly; wages—over some weeks 4s. 6d. a week, with a maximum in a considerable period of 12s.

Similar pictures were painted by other witnesses, but there is no need to repeat them; the opposition ended by admitting the facts. In doing so, they showed another aspect of the Dublin situation which must be considered in any study of Jim Larkin and his message. It demonstrates, I think, that his task was to bring about a revolutionary change in social attitudes. He himself, in his characteristic evangelical style, announced that he had come—I quote his phrase—'to preach the divine mission of discontent'. That mission, in fact, was to create a new social conscience.

The social thinking of the period is typified in a book published in 1914. It was written by Arnold Wright at the request of the Dublin Chamber of Commerce to explain to the world the employers' side of the 1913 struggle, so it is reasonable to accept it as expressing their outlook. In it Mr. Wright deals with the findings of the housing inquiry and admits quite freely that living conditions were appalling:

While it is impossible to withhold sympathy from classes so depressed as these slum dwellers of Dublin are, it cannot be overlooked that the very nature of their mode of living tends to reduce their value in the labour market.

One point upon which witness after witness insisted (during the course of giving evidence at the housing inquiry) was the physical deterioration of men who find their way into these terrible hovels. Once drawn into the abyss they speedily lose, not merely their sense of self-respect, but their capacity for sustained exertion. At the same time the thought of all that is implied in this vicious housing system in the way of demoralisation and decadence of physical powers, should make us chary of playing the role of critic to employers who have to use this damaged material.

While Mr. Wright was blaming the housing conditions as the cause of physical deterioration, the landlords were equally bitter. Their complaint was that they could not make a business proposition of letting their houses unless they crammed the tenants in in large numbers, because in smaller numbers per house the tenants were unable to afford an economic rent. This was a heads-I-win, harps-you-lose situation. In the eyes of the landlords, these slum dwellers were rent-paying units to be crammed into every available inch of space. They saw the economic problem, but failed to suspect that there was also a moral one. To Mr. Wright and the employers on whose behalf he wrote, the slum dweller, working 60 hours a week for an average wage of 16s. had lost his value in the labour market because (in Mr. Wright's words) his capacity for sustained exertion was impaired by his living conditions. He was 'damaged material'—not a unique creature made in God's image. That the 87,000 slum dwellers who were enduring all this had any rights to consideration as human|beings does not seem to have occurred to anybody. James Joyce spoke of Dublin as the centre of paralysis. It was a total paralysis, blinding conscience and soul. It remained to Jim Larkin to see the slum dweller as a human being—degraded, yet capable of nobility, perceptive, capable of living with dignity, capable, even, of music and literature. That was the message he began to address to the city at large—a message of love, delivered, one must concede, by a man swinging wildly about him with a sword.

The Irish Transport & General Workers' Union, which he formed in 1909, was designed to cater for the masses of un-skilled workers—carters, dockers, labourers, factory-hands and so on—for whom there had been no effective organization before his arrival. While the militancy of this new body was startling Dublin out of its moral and intellectual paralysis, Larkin made effective appeals to the skilled workers and the craft unions to help the unskilled men in their fight and to abandon the customary snobbery that distinguished between the bowler hat and the cloth cap. Meanwhile, because drink played its part in the degradation of the poor, he launched a private temperance campaign and succeeded, at least, to the extent of having the custom of making wages offices out of certain public houses abolished. Corruption and jobbery he attacked by frontal methods that were typical of his style—naming the offenders and prodding at them in speech after speech until he created uproar; and sometimes, let it be confessed, naming the wrong people in his enthusiasm. He thundered against low wages and bad housing in nightly harangues that mixed the vernacular with quotations from Whitman and Shelley. The masses listened spellbound, even when they didn't quite understand. James Connolly returned from America in 1910 to find the industrial world torn by strikes and lock-outs. In those furious onslaughts of Dublin's lowliest toilers he saw his watchword 'What we want is less philosophizing and more fighting' in daily operation. Soon Connolly was in the struggle too as an official of the union.

From 1908 to 1913 the business life of the city staggered from crisis to crisis, the unskilled workers in revolt, the employers fighting back, at first individually, then with attempted solidarity through their federation, which was formed in 1911. At this stage the development of simple machinery for direct negotiation might have eased the situation. Instead, however, the archaic pattern continued; the union served its demands, the employers rejected them, the men went on strike. When Larkin suggested that the employers should meet the workers' representatives for direct negotiations, it was looked on, for the most part, as further evidence of his vanity and his arrogance. The solution eventually proposed to the federation was the banning of the union altogether. This led to a head-on clash and the tragic struggle of 1913.

The battle opened in August of that year, when employees throughout the city were issued with a form and requested to sign. The document contained this sentence: 'I agree to immediately resign my membership of the Irish Transport & General Workers' Union (if a member) and I further undertake that I will not join or in any way support that union.' The document was issued indiscriminately to Transport Union members and members of various other unions.

The decision to issue it may have been based on a miscalculation, on the assumption that Larkinism could be isolated from the rest of trade unionism and liquidated separately. For some months many employers had been carrying extra staff, with the intention of using these men to replace Transport Union men if a lock-out became necessary. William Martin Murphy, the employers' spokesman, stated publicly that 'he had no apprehension that a strike would be attempted, and no fear at all—if it was attempted—that it would last a single day'.

Despite what Mr. Murphy had to say, the Transport men refused to sign the document and, as the time limit in each job expired, they were locked out. The machinery of intimidation then went into action. Police reinforcements were drafted into the city, police pensioners were called back and sworn in to do duty as gaolers, the military were alerted and stood-by in readiness. Larkinism and Society stood face to face, ready for battle.

It was at this point that Larkin's grips on the Dublin working class was revealed at its most impressive. He had proved his extraordinary power in Belfast in 1907 when he persuaded nationalist and orange workers to march together as an expression of class solidarity. He proved it again in Dublin in August 1913, when the members of thirty-two other unions in the city took their stand firmly on the side of the Larkinites and refused to sign the employers' document. This colossal expression of defiance shocked the federation. 400 firms began to lock out right, left and centre. Soon the city was paralysed and about 100,000 people faced hunger and want. They faced it for eight months. And, by and large, remained stubborn to the end.

Jim Larkin's great task, as I have said, was to create a new social conscience. His efforts, of course, were only one part of a broader struggle which was being fought the world over; in Russia through the Bolshevists, in America through the I.W.W., along the Clyde and in Liverpool and other industrial centres where liberal England was in its death throes and the the great fight between socialism and toryism was being joined. Larkin fought spectacularly. When funds ran low he rallied enormous support from the British working class as a result of a campaign in Britain. He called it, dramatically, 'The Fiery Cross Campaign'. He brought ships steaming up the Liffey with food for his locked-out followers—another dramatic gesture. It would have been easier to send the money, of course, but Larkin always chose the extravagant and the heroic. He knew that to hold 100,000 hungry people together you needed something more dramatic than a subscription list. Ships steaming in with flags, torchlight processions and bands, songs and slogans and the thunder of speeches from the windows of Liberty Hall, these were his weapons, and he calculated that a man with an empty belly would stand the pain of it better if you could succeed in filling his head full of poetry. Those who previously had nothing with which to fill out the commonplace of drab days could now march in processions, wave torches, yell out songs and cheer their own ships as they bore down the Liffey with food and good tidings. Men cannot live on poetry forever. But it is an ennobling experience to live on it for even a little while. It was Larkin's triumph to inject enough of it into a starving class to lift them off their knees and lead them out of the pit.

But he did more. His methods attracted the best spirits in Ireland to the workers' side, and as a result of 1913 the cause of the poor became identified with their larger plans for a new and free Ireland. Padraic Pearse wrote in support of the workers and showed his sympathy with Larkin in a practical way by keeping his two sons at St. Enda's. Yeats, AE, Bernard Shaw, Tom Kettle, Joseph Plunkett, Thomas MacDonagh, Eamon Ceannt, James Stephens and Padraic Colum came in on Larkins' side. Countess Markiewicz and Mrs. Sheehy Skeffington laboured in the soup kitchens of Liberty Hall and helped to feed the hungry wives and children of the strikers. There were, of course, those who disapproved. Arthur Griffith attacked Larkin bitterly in *Sinn Fein* and spoke of 'the vile and destructive methods of demagogues posing as strike leaders'. Larkin's attempt to send children of the strikers to English homes was publicly denounced. His plan to remove them for a little while from a city of hunger and want was regarded as a danger to their faith and morals. Clergy and laity patrolled the railway stations and the quaysides and snatched the children away from those who were in charge of them. Sometimes, in their zeal, they snatched the wrong children and left perfectly respectable fathers and mothers arguing desperately for the return of their offspring. Sheehy Skeffington was an active helper in the effort to get the children to England; Sir William Orpen, who used to visit Larkin's office in Liberty Hall, has left a picture of Skeffington back from one of these engagements wrapped in a blanket for decency's sake—his clothes had been torn off him. But perhaps Larkin himself put this sorry interlude in proper perspective. 'It's a poor religion', he said, 'that won't stand up to a fortnight's holidays'.

When the struggle ended, the right of a hitherto forgotten class to consideration in any plan for a free Ireland had been planted firmly in the minds of the nation's leaders. In addition, the Citizen Army existed, pledged to the cause of a workers' republic. 'God Save Ireland' was the slogan of the middle class nationalist who dreamed of restoring to Kathleen Ni Hoolihaun her four green fields. 'God Save The People' answered the leaders of the Citizen Army, who to paraphrase James Connolly, were not prepared to destroy British capitalism simply for the sake of replacing it by Irish capitalism. They had more revolutionary plans than that, which they hoped to realise through the Irish Citizen Army, formed during the 1913 strike and reconstituted in 1914, with Larkin as its first commandant, to fight for the establishment of a workers' republic. Later Connolly's influence brought both nationalists and Citizen Army men together in a closer understanding and in 1916 they fought side by side.

By this time, however, Larkin had gone to America, to raise funds, as he announced, to rebuild the union and to tell American labour of Irish problems and methods. While there he barely escaped hanging at the hands of hired thugs on a couple of occasions, and eventually he was sentenced to ten years' penal servitude for what the court termed 'Criminal Syndicalism.' He served three years in Sing Sing before being released by order of Governor Al Smith in 1923.

For the first time since 1914 Larkin found himself with permission and means of returning to Ireland. His journey was a progress of triumph. American workers lined the docks to cheer him off; at Southampton the British workers turned up in their thousands to pay him honour. In Dublin the streets from Westland Row station to Liberty Hall were packed with people; young men unyoked the wagonette in which he was travelling and themselves dragged it through the streets. Five bands marched in the procession and the people sang strike songs and shouted the slogans of 1913.

This high moment of triumph was the prelude to a bitter split. The union had grown enormously strong during his absence. Its part in the 1913 struggle, the fame of Larkin's exploits, Connolly's execution in 1916, its association with 1916 through many of its officials and members and through the Irish Citizen Army, all these things endeared it to the ordinary people. But to Larkin's mind things were not well. He had planned to return with a food ship for the relief of dependants of political prisoners, as a prelude to a campaign for unity and an end to fratricidal strike. The executive of the union had refused. He had not forgotten the hostility of Arthur Griffith and distrusted the outlook of his successors in power. The policy of wage cuts which the government was pursuing seemed to him to be proof enough that labour's share in the philosophy of the new state was being gobbled up by the nationalists. In fact he had expressed this fear in letters from America after the rising. 'The gang here', he wrote (meaning the Irish Americans) 'are more fearful of *our* movement getting ahead in Eire than if Johnny Bull played the same game as in '98. They make out Arthur G. as a Godgiven saint and statesman. Nobody in Ireland did anything but Sinn Fein. Connolly and the other boys all recanted socialism and labour and were good Sinn Feiners. My God, it is sickening'. Larkin felt that the union was not acting forcefully enough to put the case of labour and socialism to the Irish people. His view was the same as that expressed in 1919 by Sean O'Casey when he predicted in his 'Story of the Citizen Army' that 'Labour would probably have to fight Sinn Fein'.

Although Larkin was still general secretary, there were members on the executive committee who were antagonistic to him. Besides, he was never a man to allow an executive to overrule him. He provoked a legal battle for control of the union, declaring the executive to be illegally elected. He lost and was expelled from the union he had formed fourteen years before. Within a few months of his triumphal return Larkin, an undischarged bankrupt, was expelled by his colleagues and hated by the government. The last prophet of the workers' republic was a national outcast. But a penniless Larkin had assets no law or committee could strip him of. They were courage, a magnetic personality, and a superb gift of oratory. Within months he had rallied his old guard of carters and dockers, founded another union, and was leading strikes with undefeated vigour and recklessness. Gradually he assumed leadership once more in the eclipsed world of gaslight and tenement and gradually he won his way into public life. Pearse was dead and Connolly was dead and Skeffington, and all the other great hearts who had room for his passionate views of an Ireland of the people. He fought his way alone, re-establishing his influence through the Dublin Trades Council and the activities of his new union—the Workers' Union of Ireland. He became a city councillor and on two occasions a deputy of Dail Éireann. In the nineteen-forties he led a campaign against the Wages Standstill Order and succeeded in forcing amending legislation. His last large scale efforts were to help in the foundation of a union for agricultural workers and the formulation of a demand for a fortnight's annual leave for manual workers, which after a fourteen weeks' strike was generally conceded.

In the course of forty years of social agitation Jim Larkin earned a reputation which was universal. Yet he was no doctrinaire revolutionary in the Continental sense and he was no great theorist. R. M. Fox in his biography, speaks of him as a socialist of the old British school, a description which is near enough to the mark, but still inadequate. Perhaps the employers of Dublin found the best name for his movement when they labelled it Larkinism. His lifelong concern was not with theory, but with the immediate needs of the underprivileged—the sweated men, the struggling mothers, the little children born to a life of drudgery in a sunless world. In his efforts to help them he was sometimes arrogant, sometimes unfair to colleagues and often rash beyond the justification of his most indulgent admirers. He could fling a terrible phrase at the employers—'You'll crucify Christ no longer in this town' and then turn with equal venom on his religious critics. Once, when an eminent churchman warned the people against him he said: 'Hell has no terrors for me. I've lived there. Thirty-six years of hunger and poverty

have been my portion. The mother who bore me had to starve
and work, and the father I loved had to fight for a living. I
knew what it was to work when I was nine years old. They
can't terrify me with hell. Better to be in hell with Dante and
Davitt than to be in heaven with Carson and Murphy'. This,
no doubt, is emotive argument, but it makes a point that is
larger than the measure of its logic. Larkin was adept at returning bombs before they had time to explode.

For the rest, he was a man of sober habits and few wants and
he walked throughout life, as he himself said, 'always in the fear
of God, but never in the fear of any man'. When he died in 1947,
he left behind him some personal articles, a little furniture and
£4 10s. od. in money, the balance of his weekly wages.

1946 had seen the setting up of the Labour Court, which
symbolised the victory of trade unionism in its fight for a
respected and influential place in the social and economic life
of modern Ireland. Here was the beginning of a new stage in
labour relations, with its machinery for direct negotiation and
conciliation representing new privileges for trade unionism,
but also placing on its shoulders new responsibilities. Jim
Larkin was the last of the great militants, and with his funeral
on that bleak day in February of 1947, when thousands stood
in the slush and the cold to bid him farewell, an era of titanic
struggle moved peacefully to an end.

JAMES PLUNKET.

THE SUM OF THINGS

In Thomas Russell's unpublished diaries, which the United Irish leader kept in the early seventeen-nineties, there are a number of jottings, thoughts put down in a rough and unpolished state. They are reflections on what Disraeli called 'the two nations'—the rich and the poor. Here is one of them:

> We see the vices of the rich in so far from being considered as shameful that some are made honourable. Whence this but from the rich making laws? Property put before life. Property must be altered in some measure.

Such reflections were not to the liking of the romantic word-painters—we can scarcely call them historians—of the nineteenth century. The social and economic thinking of the more advanced United Irishman was an embarrassing colour in an otherwise ideal portrait of an Irish patriot. So the historical portraitist covered it with a thick coat of green varnish. It was Connolly who stripped away the varnish and revealed the real colours beneath. The crude oleographs may still be in circulation, but it is no longer possible to claim that they are faithful representations of the originals.

What then is the significance of Russell's reflections? Surely it is that he, and others such as Tone, Jemmy Hope, Emmett and the brothers Sheares, realized that a purely political change which left social and economic relationships undisturbed would never secure in Ireland the greatest happiness of the greatest number. If there is a common motivation to be found in the lives of all the men in this series it is that property must not be put before life, and that in consequence it must be altered.

We should not make the mistake of attributing to these early radicals of the United Irishmen any planned solution to the problem of poverty, still less any socialist solution. But we can say that they perceived, even if indistinctly, what Connolly saw clearly a century later when he declared political and social freedom 'to be two sides of the one great principle'. The temper of the times gave primacy to the claims of political freedom, and when they were silenced so were those of social freedom also.

As Ireland entered the new century economic and social questions assumed an importance rivalling on occasions that of political issues. William Thompson set himself to answer them. As an improving landlord he was a child of the eighteenth century, as a supporter of catholic emancipation and an advocate of women's rights he shared in the generous enthusiasms generated by the French revolution, but when he analysed the economic and social structure of society he was a man of the nineteenth century, the century of full-scale industrialisation. It was unusual that a landlord should concern himself with economic studies, it was remarkable that he should draw conclusions so opposed to the interests of his own class. Thompson argued that the labourer was entitled to the full value of his labour. The system of private property denied him half of it, lessened his incentive to produce and hence acted as a brake on production generally. It was responsible for a society marked by extremes of wealth and poverty and the resultant inequality diminished the sum of human happiness without proportionately increasing the happiness of the rich. It encouraged luxury and viciousness among the rich and tended to infect the whole of society—a moral reflection which recalls Russell's remark that some of the vices of the men of property (he mentions gambling and duelling among others) were considered honourable.

Thompson's concern with questions of equitable distribution stamps him as remarkably far-seeing, not only as a forerunner of Karl Marx but as an economist in advance of his times, for has not the central problem of social economics in our own day been that of distribution? Unlike many early socialists he did not propose the restoration of a golden age on the basis of a crude agrarian socialism, but contended that if society were properly organized industrialisation could lead to an increase in human happiness. A society of independent producers was merely an attempt to equalize the old domestic system and threw away the gains of the new techniques, but a co-operative commonwealth would utilize them and as well assure equitable distribution.

Thompson was distinguished from Robert Owen by his insistence that the mass of the people must lift themselves out of poverty by their own exertions; they could not rely on the benevolence of the rich to hasten its abolition. He contended that the rich as a class, though there might be individual exceptions, would oppose the coming of an egalitarian society. Wolfe Tone concluded that the men of property might be unreliable in any struggle for liberty and that merchants did not make good revolutionaries. Russell made the same observation, adding that when the people saw this they would in time feel both their injuries and their strength; they would 'do it themselves and then *adieu* property'. Is it fanciful to see in Thompson's contention the result of his experiences in Ireland, where the gulf between rich and poor was so great? Perhaps, but it is certain that in this as in other matters Thompson stated with clarity and precision what some United Irish leaders felt instinctively.

The cotton-spinner John Doherty realized the injuries of his class and its potential strength. His energies were spent initially in attempts to form general trade unions. The industrial expansion which had begun during the second half of the eighteenth century in England gathered momentum early in the next century and drew into the towns great numbers to work in the trades using power-driven machinery, especially in textiles. There was no similar development in Ireland, where craft industry ruled, except Belfast's short-lived cotton industry. Had Doherty stayed in this country instead of following cotton-spinning to Manchester he would have found few opportunities for trade union organization, as well as less work and lower wages. In the circumstances, which included growing population pressure on an inefficient agricultural system, it is understandable that the more energetic spirits among Irish workers should have gone to England. Doherty was but one of the earliest of Irish emigrants who became leaders of the British labour movement.

Recent historians of that movement have taken up Connolly's task of rescuing Doherty from oblivion, for they recognize the importance of the Donegal-born pioneer. He saw two objectives for trade union organization, the protection and improvement of working conditions and, since he was an Owenite socialist, the creation of a new social order. He showed realism in deciding to build a strong union to cover the cotton spinners of the two islands and in using it as a nucleus for a congress of all the trades, the National Association for the Protection of Labour, founded in 1830.

He showed vision in attempting to create, almost forty years before the founding of the Trade Union Congress, a body which would concentrate working-class strength and could aid the movement towards a co-operative commonwealth. And his several ventures in journalism, notably, *The United Trades Co-operative Journal* and *The Voice of the People*, had the same double objective, and incidentally anticipated Chartist papers such as the *Northern Star*. A just assessment of Doherty's work will emphasise, not the failure of his more ambitious plans in unfavourable historical circumstances, but their prophetic nature. Nor should it be forgotten that even after the dissolution of the National Association for the Protection of Labour, individual unions were sufficiently strong to survive and recover much of their strength after the passing of the 1832 Reform Act.

The Irish contribution so far had been to the development
of socialist theory and trade union organisation; with the rise
of Chartism it was extended to active working-class politics.
The potent social and economic grievances that gave rise to
it—the three high peaks of the movement in 1839, 1842 and
1848 coincided with trade depressions—resulted in demands
that were primarily political, as the six points of the Charter
itself show. In this great agitation, which in its mass basis and
many of its methods resembles O'Connell's repeal movement
of the same period, Feargus O'Connor and Bronterre O'Brien
were leaders. When every allowance is made for its impractical
aspects Chartism remains a passionate expression of the working
population's desire for a democratic society, a society in which
the rich would not always make the laws.

Neither in membership nor in interests was Chartism exclusively English. It had support in Ireland, in particular in
Dublin, and, despite O'Connell's hostility, its leaders endorsed
repeal demands. In retrospect it can be seen that O'Connell
and O'Connor had certain characteristics in common other
than their middle-class origins. Both were lawyers and speakers
with immense popular appeal, one leading peasants and the
other industrial workers in mass demonstrations. Both enjoyed
the power their oratory gave them and both gave way, at
Clontarf and at Kennington Common, when their meetings
were banned by the authorities.

But their differences were profound. O'Connor condemned
O'Connell's compact with the whigs, his support of the new
poor law and his denunciation of trade unions. Their disagree-
ments were not confined to objectives. Though the repeal
leader might be called 'The King of the Beggars' and O'Connor
might address himself to the 'fustian jackets and the unshorn
chins', O'Connell refused O'Connor's suggested alliance of
the English and Irish democracies. The United Irishmen would
not have baulked at such a proposal; the Dublin society made
the Scottish revolutionary democrat Thomas Muir a member
and kept up a steady correspondence with English, Scottish
and French societies. O'Connor and O'Brien were of a like
mind, O'Brien in particular not hesitating to draw lessons
from revolutionary France. Indeed Irish democratic leaders
in this tradition were always ready to maintain fraternal relations
with reformers and egalitarians of other countries while insisting
on their own national tradition.

It may be argued plausibly that James Fintan Lalor should
find no place in this series. Connolly calls him 'the Irish apostle
of revolutionary socialism', an epithet which cannot properly
be applied to him. Lalor's revolutionary temper, combined
with a certain vagueness of language, misled the author of

Labour in Irish history. Lalor's concern was with the tenant farmers; he was anxious above all to prevent them sinking into the hopeless condition of landless labourers. He desired to see them transformed into a 'numerous and efficient agricultural yeomanry' before any extension of industry took place; he was silent on the plight of the urban workers, still small in numbers, whose grievances were little known. Yet he may be admitted if for no other reason that he was a name of power for Davitt, and, even if misleadingly, for Connolly. Nor must it be forgotten that this son of a prosperous tenant farmer, unlike O'Connell, maintained relations with English Chartists and suggested that one should be an editor of the proposed successor to the *Irish Felon*.

Michael Davitt was the son of an evicted Mayo peasant, one of the many thousands driven off the land and compelled to find a living in English industry. His early experiences, the loss of his right arm, a prison sentence of nine years for Fenian activities, all might have filled another man with unrelenting hatred for everything English. His generous nature, which always admitted the claims of a common humanity, prevented him becoming an Anglophobe; he never equated the individual with the system. In his speech before *The Times* commission he acknowledged his debt to English democracy:

> The first man after my father whom I ever heard denouncing landlordism, not only in Ireland but in England, was Ernest Jones, who had himself been once imprisoned as an agitator: the first lesson I ever learned in the doctrine of liberty was from English and not from Irish history.

Ernest Jones was a link with the Chartists, for he was one of Feargus O'Connor's principal lieutenants. O'Connor had wanted an alliance of Irish peasants and English urban workers to right the wrongs of both. Davitt urged a not dissimilar policy in more favourable circumstances. He proposed to link the cause of the Irish agricultural labourers and urban workers, two classes hitherto neglected, with the tenant farmers' cause; to direct a revived land agitation towards nationalisation; to make the demand for Irish independence one of the aims of the British labour movement and to have the Irish party the representative of their interests in parliament.

Davitt's own efforts to assist and educate the British labour movement were frowned upon by Parnell, as was his assistance to the labour movement in Ireland. It was ironical that Parnell should turn in 1891 to the Dublin workers for support in his hour of need; it was even more ironical that after 1900 spokesmen of the Irish parliamentary party should, following years of comparative indifference, assure successive congresses of the Irish T.U.C. that there was no need for a separate labour party as one already existed—the Irish party. Though Davitt never succeeded in effecting a final junction between the various forces, and though his own inclination was to a 'lib-lab' rather than a fully socialist position, his services to the working-classes of Great Britain and Ireland were constant and un-wearying; they were recognised at his death in the tributes paid by the most diverse labour organisations and leaders.

Davitt's direct experience of industrial life was brief, and if he gave generous help to the labour movement it was as a sympathetic ally, not a member. All three of the remaining leaders in this series were born into the industrial working class and their lives, like Doherty's, were shaped by it.

William Walker stands apart. An able official of his own craft union, he had only a limited success as a political labour leader in the difficult terrain of his native city. Belfast with its complex pattern of segregation has craved wary walking for the trade union organiser; for the advocate of independent labour representation it has required the wisdom of serpents rather than the harmlessness of doves. The fortunes of labour in that city have varied inversely with the rise and fall of the home rule barometer. It was in the relative calm of the period between the South African war and the third home rule bill that Walker made his mark. Even the very mild fluctuation caused by the Irish Councils proposal of 1907 affected his chances adversely.

It is difficult to assess accurately Walker's contribution to the labour movement, whether in Belfast, in Ireland or in Great Britain. As a young man he had assisted in the formation of a number of semi-skilled and general unions, but when he became an official of his own union he virtually restricted his trade union activities to it. He was several times a delegate to the Irish T.U.C., and even president one year, but he regarded it at best as an indifferent substitute—he regretted the circumstances which had led to the successive departures of the Irish and Scots from the British T.U.C. His political labour activities, at least in his later years, seem to have been conditioned in part by his own ambitions. He became vice-chairman of the British Labour Party in 1911 but withdrew his candidature for the chair the following year when he left politics for national insurance, so that his career in the British as opposed to the Irish labour movement ended with a question mark.

Walker contended repeatedly that there was complete identity of interest between British and Irish workers and that in consequence Irish labour should be part of the more powerful movement. This was a very different proposition from that put forward either by O'Connor or Davitt, for it took no account of the claims of separate national identity or of the still unexhausted driving force of agrarian discontent; it was the product of an urban, even of a local environment. In an Irish context his assertion that he was 'a Unionist in politics' labelled him a colonial in nationalist eyes; his answers to the Belfast Protestant Association's questions, questions skilfully ignored by his opponent, proved that he was unable to rise above the limitations of his immediate surroundings. His importance lies less in what he achieved than in what he represented—the desire on the part of unionist workers to combine the constitutional views of the Ulster Unionist Council with the social policies of the British Labour Party.

Walker and Connolly, who were near contemporaries, died in their forties. Walker has been forgotten, but an ironic fate has overtaken Connolly, for he has undergone the same transformation as the United Irishmen. His death in the Easter rising has depersonalised him, as did the death of Russell in 1803, making him a symbol of a country's fight for independence, and obscuring in the process his social ideas. For many the militant nationalist *is* Connolly, the international socialist an aberration.

In his Glasgow *Forward* controversy with Walker Connolly made it abundantly clear that internationalism for him meant 'a free federation of free peoples'. His desire for an Irish labour party that would preserve its separate identity, while at the same time exchanging literature and speakers with the British party, was a reasonable corollary, and gained added cogency from the apparently near emergence of a separate Irish parliament. Part of Connolly's irritation with Walker arose from the urgent need for unity and the utilisation of all labour forces if labour were to have a strong voice in the new legislature. Part of it stems from his recognition that they, or at least their organisations, had much in common. This was true even of controversial subjects; both for instance disliked clerical interference in politics and both agreed that education should be public in the American sense, publicly financed and controlled by popularly-elected bodies, a view held by Davitt and his predecessors. On general social and economic objectives there was a considerable measure of agreement, though Connolly's conception of a workers' republic was more far-reaching than Walker's municipally centred socialism.

In terms of aims realised Connolly may seem to have accomplished little. As a trade union organiser he was set extremely difficult tasks; in Belfast he had to contend with sectarian differences and inter-union rivalries, yet he succeeded in improving the lot of mill girls and dockers. In Dublin he was faced with the heavy task of building up a union exhausted by eight months of a struggle in which no quarter was shown. The various political labour organisations that he started never took firm root. He was however responsible for adding a political wing to the Irish T.U.C., but this had hardly been done when war held up its growth and diverted his own energies to preparations for the Easter rising. He did not live to see accomplished what he had so strenuously opposed and feared, the partition of his country.

A historian may be forgiven if he considers that Connolly made his greatest contribution to the Irish labour movement in his writings. His vigour and directness, and his analytical power, make other labour journalists seem vague, sentimental and verbose. His *Labour in Irish history*, with its tribute to Marx, 'the first scientific socialist', is an astonishing work for a man whose life allowed him opportunities for self-education and research only at the cost of severe sacrifice; if some of his judgments must be modified, the book still remains a pioneer work of great value.

James Larkin, a younger contemporary of Connolly and Walker, is a figure from the heroic age of trade unionism. From 1907 to 1914 he dominated and transformed the Irish labour movement, infusing it with some of his own gospel of divine discontent. He brought into its ranks the general labourer whose existence until his arrival had scarcely been recognised. A close examination of his work, first as official of the National Union of Dock Labourers and later of the Irish Transport and General Workers' Union, shows that he organised skilfully, gathering members steadily and negotiating with considerable ability. But when he felt that a crisis was reached he would not give way. Employers at that time accepted, generally speaking, the existence of trades (i.e., skilled) unions, and were prepared to deal with them, but they adopted quite a different attitude towards the organisation of labourers. Larkin was determined to establish the right of the labourer to join a union, and was prepared, if it were not conceded, to invoke his doctrine of 'tainted goods' and use the weapon of the sympathetic strike. These tactics called forth his superb gifts as an agitator and incidentally created in the minds of his enemies the image of Larkin as a destructive force. It is true that the organisation proper suffered in these struggles and that the work of his successors consisted of consolidation before expansion, but without Larkin's initial efforts there would have been nothing to build on. Even when employers were techni-cally victorious they gradually came to realise that there could be no permanent return to the old order of things.

If Larkin wished to destroy he also wished to rebuild. He was a declared socialist, a founder member of an early I.L.P.

branch, and both before and after his stay in the United States took part in Irish labour politics. But until relatively late in life he was constantly frustrated, either by involvement in the long series of industrial disputes before 1914 or in inter-union struggles after 1923. His desire for a socialist order of society was strong, even if he saw it in less precise detail than his fellow-unionist Connolly. Unlike him he left no body of doctrine—he had not Connolly's powers of detachment or analysis—but what he wrote is still worth reading for its telling phrases, its hatred of cruelty and oppression and its passionate desire for justice, as the files of his paper, the *Irish Worker*, bear witness.

The active lives of the leaders in this series together cover a century and a half. It is inevitable that over such a stretch of time with its changing historical situations there must be diversity of outlook among men possessing strong and distinctive personalities. Yet when all qualifications are made, a common conviction remains to bind them together, a conviction that human society must be democratic, not only politically but socially. Mr. Lynch when beginning this series, cited Tone's statement about the men of no property; I have quoted the conviction of Tone's closest friend, Thomas Russell, that property must not be put before life. The united social democracy envisaged by Connolly as an embodiment of the sum of things, the common weal, is essentially an amplification of that conviction.

J. W. BOYLE.

THE THOMAS DAVIS LECTURES

Series published by THE MERCIER PRESS